McMAS
&
COMMANDER

THE BUSINESS OF WINNING

JOHN McMASTER

WITH DAVID CHRISTIE, NEIL MARTIN AND ROBIN McAUSLAN

FOREWORD BY GRAHAM HUNTER

First Edition.
First published 2023

Published by:
Morgan Lawrence Publishing Services Limited
Ridge House Annexe
16 Main Ridge West
Boston
Lincolnshire
PE21 6QQ
www.morganlawrence.co.uk
email: info@morganlawrence.co.uk
Company number: 12910264

ISBN: 9781838232986

A CIP catalogue record is available for this book from the British Library.

Photographs are courtesy of:
AFC Heritage Trust - The Aberdeen Collection, PA Images/ Alamy Stock Photo, Trinity Mirror/Mirror Pix, Allstar Picture Library Limited, Greenock Telegraph, Eugene Jean Méhat, Bob Thomas, Getty Images.

Cover design by LCgrapix. Cover photos by AFC Heritage Trust.

Printed and bound in Bulgaria
by Pulsio Print.

Contents

Foreword by Graham Hunter 5

Introduction 9

Chapter 1 – Pendulum 13

Chapter 2 – Growing Up 17

Chapter 3 – A Family Man 29

Chapter 4 – Leading The Way 33

Chapter 5 – The Long Road 45

Chapter 6 – More Than Just The Boss 51

Chapter 7 – No Prizes For Coming Second 67

Chapter 8 – Getting Emotional 79

Chapter 9 – A Change Is Gonna Come 89

Chapter 10 – Got To Get A Message To You 99

Chapter 11 – You Got The Power 105

Chapter 12 – You Have To Admit It's Getting Better 115

Chapter 13 – From Gibshill To Gothenburg 125

Chapter 14 – The Super Cup 137

Chapter 15 – Coming Home 141

Chapter 16 – Reflection 151

Chapter 17 – The Business Parallels 155

Epilogue – Dewy Eyed Romanticism 165

Acknowledgements 169

Thank You To Our Sponsors 171

- Aberdeen Football Club Heritage Trust 172
- McLeod+Aitken 173
- Just Employment Law 174
- Pier Solutions 175

Statistics And Honours 176

Meet The Writers 177

- Robin McAuslan 178
- David Christie 179
- Neil Martin 180

McLeod+Aitken

FOREWORD BY
Graham Hunter

THERE ARE ONLY FOURTEEN MEN in the history of football who've lifted two European trophies for a Scottish club, and the mighty John McMaster is one of them.

Fergie (Sir Alex now, but if you were a Dandy back in 1978 when he joined us, he was Fergie then and he's Fergie now) always used to say that Peter Weir was the one who, on European nights, elevated Aberdeen with his special balance, trickery and ability to tie a defender (hello, Mick Mills) in knots.

True. But Johnny Mac (Spammer to his teammates) elevated us too, because there have been few players in Scottish football history with such brilliant left-footed distribution of the ball. John was very special.

And not simply because he was technically gifted off his left boot.

This is a guy who properly understood football, did simple things simply but then produced visionary, intelligent actions which made winning easier for other teammates to whom he supplied the ball with a ribbon tied on the pass or cross.

We are talking, too, about a tough, funny guy who'd been raised the old way—amongst folks who truly knew how to work properly hard for a living.

Where danger and professional pride went hand in hand: shipyard people.

Raised playing from dawn till dusk with a ball—learning the tricks and the savvy that street footballers had.

The ball was precious—not precious like Pep Guardiola thinks about possession, but precious because actually affording the price of a football was a privilege that not all could manage.

But then '*owning*' the ball once you were playing in a gang of ten, fifteen, twenty mates guaranteed that you were cock of the walk. If you were good in possession, knew how to get it, knew how to use it, then you had status.

Every football that John McMaster ever kicked knew that he was its friend, knew that a guy with ability and vision had taken charge.

There'll be a lot in this book about Alexander Chapman Ferguson.

Fergie was also from shipyard stock. The fact that Johnny Mac and he shared roots and values, came from tough, proud stock where a job was only done if it was done properly, was already bound to tie them together when they met.

The fact that Fergie liked to use his left peg, admired those who could ping the ball, meant that inheriting John from Billy McNeill was a gift from the heavens.

However, the way that John explains Fergie's attitude, decisions and support at the time of his greatest need should impress you all over again.

I remember queuing overnight in autumn 1980 to try and get a hugely prized ticket to watch the Dandies play Liverpool in what was only the second European Cup tie that Aberdeen had been in during my lifetime.

What left me far, far more upset than losing to the eventual European champions, thanks to Terry McDermott's goal, was the way that Ray Kennedy injured John.

It's for the author to tell the tale—the doubt, the pain, the long rehab and Fergie's part in it all. But what I want to emphasise strongly is that John should NOT, under any circumstances, be remembered principally for that incident.

Not only did he return, having missed out on a hugely deserved Scotland call-up, which would have come his way immediately after the Liverpool tie; he re-deployed from midfield to left back and played with such brilliance, such reliability, such wit and cleverness that he is, without any question, in my all-time Dons XI.

It should stick in everyone's mind that Pittodrie's greatest ever night, that monumental 3-2 win over Bayern Munich, had John's style stamped all over it.

The dummy argument with Gordon Strachan, which led to big Scooby McLeish nodding home the equaliser and then John's long ball into the box, which led to Eric Black feeding wee Johnny Hewitt's brilliant winner off the bar.

And I want to share something over and above the years and years of absolute class that John brought to our mighty club on the pitch.

When I was at the ceremony for Sir Alex's statue in spring 2022, John leaned over, tapped me on the shoulder and asked how my dad was keeping.

He'd never met Graham Hunter Snr, a fifty year season ticket holder at the Home of Football, but John had heard that my mother had died and Dad, suffering from Alzheimer's, was on his own.

A couple of months later, this magnificent man drove up from Greenock and took all his shirts, tracksuits, mementos and medals up to Bieldside to share three hours of magical memories and anecdotes with my father.

A guy who'd shouted and applauded his appreciation for John since he joined in 1974, drowned out only by Buff Hardie, my dad's best friend and perpetual Pittodrie companion.

But still a guy John had never even met.

Priceless. Generous. Typical.

I'll never tell any of you why John now only refers to me as 'Pablo', but I will tell you this: John McMaster is a giant of a man—funny, talented, tough, smart, loyal, kind and a winner.

John—we love you.

INTRODUCTION

TO MANY PEOPLE, Mark Robins' FA Cup third round winning goal in 1990 against Nottingham Forest saved Alex Ferguson's Manchester United career; it started his path to greatness. After four trophyless years, Fergie was under ever-increasing pressure and his ability as a manager was supposedly in doubt. What he achieved after that, though, is now very well known.

He won an incredible 37 trophies: 13 English Premier League titles, 9 FA Charity/Community Shields, 5 FA Cups, 4 Football League Cup wins, 2 UEFA Champions Leagues, 1 European Cup Winners' Cup, 1 European Super Cup, 1 Intercontinental Cup and 1 FIFA Club World Cup—and that is only just scratching the surface of his achievements as manager of Manchester United.

Whether you like the game of football or not, whether you follow Manchester United or not, Sir Alex Ferguson is considered one of the greatest managers in the game and a name that is known all over the world.

His leadership techniques are widely recognised as a key factor in United's success, but not so much is mentioned of his triumphs at Aberdeen Football Club prior to his move to the then underachieving English giants. In truth, Ferguson's journey to greatness began long before Mark Robins kick-started Manchester United's domination of the English game.

Not that his road to greatness started at Aberdeen Football Club either, but it was there that his methods clearly came to the fore and the Business of Winning trophies really took off. Whilst at Aberdeen Football Club he won three Scottish

League titles, four Scottish Cups, one Scottish League Cup, one Drybrough Cup, one European Cup Winners' Cup and one European Super Cup. All that in just eight years with a club that, prior to Ferguson's arrival, had just a handful of honours to its name.

I was there when he walked through the door in 1978, and I was with him through thick and thin until we both left in 1986. I experienced first-hand the Boss (as I call him to this day) and his leadership and management skills that took Aberdeen Football Club from virtual anonymity to becoming a global presence in world football.

I am one of the 'Gothenburg Greats', so named after our European Cup Winners' Cup victory against Real Madrid in May 1983. At the time of publication, Aberdeen remains the last Scottish side to beat Real Madrid.

This book is both a look back at my life in football and beyond, an insight into how Sir Alex Ferguson brought his leadership skills to Aberdeen, a fishing community in the northeast of Scotland that was on its way to becoming Britain's oil capital. I've looked at this with my co-writers, all of whom have successful business backgrounds, and picked out the key aspects of Fergie's methods that apply equally well in the business world. More than that, it is an opportunity to follow the Fergie model for self-development and success.

In this book I tell you all about my journey under the Boss, including the highs and lows of my career. It is a book packed full of humorous stories around football, but it is much more than that; it also features stories of the unique leadership style and vision that drove the Business of Winning. With the help of my colleagues, I have also looked at those leadership skills that are parallel to running a business.

When I left my hometown of Greenock, on the West Coast of Scotland, in 1972, aged 17, giving up my apprenticeship as a plumber in Scott's shipyard, little did I know what was ahead of me. I didn't even know where Aberdeen was at the time! But I was determined to give it a go and try to become a professional footballer with a big club like Aberdeen Football Club.

It was a dream come true for a young lad in the 1970s. All I had ever dreamed of was becoming a professional footballer. My brother, Andrew, had encouraged me to play from an early age, and all the boys from Poplar Street, where I lived, played football—everybody did back then. No matter what the weather was like or whatever else was happening, we always ended up playing football in the street, in the close, up the hill. In fact, anywhere at all.

We all gave ourselves pretend names of players, be it from Celtic, Rangers, Manchester United, Liverpool, Chelsea, Leeds or Aston Villa; they all had Scottish International players in their teams at that time. I played in the street, for my school and Boys' Brigade teams, later progressing to the local under 16 and under 18s clubs, and then up to Aberdeen, where I became a full-time professional footballer.

What a journey that was. I probably never realised how good I really was at football until the arrival of Lisbon Lion Billy McNeill, as Aberdeen manager in 1977, and then subsequently with the Boss taking over from him a year later and turning us into winners.

This is an inspirational and true story that is personal to me and my family but told in a manner that I hope will be of interest to Aberdeen supporters, fans of the Boss, and also those with an interest in football in general. It also provides great insight into the methods that Sir Alex used that can be replicated to drive a business to be successful through great but simple leadership techniques and resilience.

What I think is unique is that this story takes you on my journey, yet allows you to draw your own conclusions as to how one man, the Boss, inspired me as an individual and motivated the squad to success; how he managed a successful business and boosted the city of Aberdeen's status around the globe.

This fascinating insight will take a look at how the Business of Winning was so evident at Aberdeen Football Club and how the Business of Winning created the building blocks for his future success at Manchester United.

CHAPTER 1
Pendulum

WEDNESDAY, 22 OCTOBER 1980 was the night that one of the great football teams came calling to Pittodrie, home of Aberdeen Football Club. As reigning champions of Scotland, Aberdeen had qualified for the European Cup, a much tougher competition than its successor the Champions League, because you had to win your domestic title in order to qualify. Finishing second in the league wasn't enough, let alone fourth. Liverpool, the champions of England, had a side littered with world class stars, including Alan Hansen, Graeme Souness, Ian Rush and Kenny Dalglish. They were aiming to lift the European Cup for the third time in five seasons.

I lined up for Aberdeen in what should have been one of the greatest nights of my career, the Battle of Britain in the European Cup, but it started badly and went downhill rapidly. Within five minutes we were a goal down after a wonderful finish from Liverpool's Terry McDermott. Their goal was made slightly easier for them as we had been temporarily reduced to ten men at the time because I was doubled over at the side of the pitch throwing up, having caught Sammy Lee's elbow in my face a few moments earlier.

On the quarter hour mark, it was all over for me as I suffered a potentially career-ending knee injury following a tackle by Ray Kennedy. I had been on a diagonal run from the halfway line towards the left side of the box when I entered Ray's territory, and bang, down I went. The tackle was brutal enough, even if the referee didn't think it warranted a booking, but my studs got caught in the turf, so as my body twisted from the knee up, my leg stayed straight, planted in the ground. Something had to give, and that something turned out to be my inside medial ligament.

My right leg was in agony and the damage threatened my entire career, maybe even my ability to walk, although that probably wasn't evident straight away. The immediate diagnosis from the physio—as it so often was in those days—was to "Give it five mins and see how it is!" But that was the end of the match for me, and it would be a long time before I kicked a ball again!

As the Liverpool game neared its conclusion, and a first leg defeat from which there would be no coming back, I was sitting in the dressing room dealing with the severe pain caused by the injury, cursing Ray Kennedy upside down. There had been no apology on the park, and despite the impact that the injury had on me over the next 18 months, there were no get well soon cards from my opponent either! To be fair, at that point no one had any idea how bad the injury actually was. Even the club doctor, Mr Cathro, thought I might be OK—he slapped me on the injured knee and said I'd be fit for the return match after having a cortisone injection! That was how things were done in those days.

After an uncomfortable night at home, I returned to the stadium the following morning for another examination by the physio before eventually an appointment was made for me to go to hospital. By now the reality of the situation was starting to dawn on me. When I was on my way to hospital to be assessed, I knew it wasn't looking good. My leg was swinging like a pendulum, as the surgeon, Mr Tom Scotland, later described it in the hospital. Now, I'm no doctor but even I knew that wasn't a good sign!

I was operated on the next morning as the surgeon tried his best to repair the damage. And the damage was bad. Nowadays, thanks to medical advances, a lot of these injuries can be fixed through a less invasive process called keyhole surgery, but back then, the only option was to cut my leg open. The muscles needed to be rearranged to support my knee, and 28 stitches were required to seal the wound. The Boss was the first person to hear how bad the injury truly was. He was waiting at the hospital to see how I was when I came around from the operation and, being genuinely concerned for his employee, he went to see the surgeon to get an update from him. The prognosis wasn't good; the surgeon told Sir Alex that my knee was so badly damaged that it was unlikely I would ever play football again!

It was at that point, and I didn't know this until talking to the Boss many years later, that the ability of the man to understand individual people came to the fore. His instant reaction to the surgeon was to instruct him not to tell me that my career was in doubt. As he always took the time to talk to his staff, get to know them individually and understand their strengths and weaknesses, he realised that receiving such devastating news would cause me great problems psychologically. I was a bit of a worrier, had a mortgage, a wife and two young kids, and he recognised that what I needed was hope and encouragement. I needed a feeling of safety and security.

When I awoke, the first person I saw was the Boss, which in itself was a fantastic boost. The sense that someone in his position was taking the time to show how much he cared about me gave me great heart and also helped to cement a huge feeling of loyalty. He kicked into action straight away. "Listen, son, don't you worry about anything. I've already spoken to Katy (my wife) and let her know everything is being looked after, so she knows that she doesn't need to worry about the family and the mortgage and so on. Here's what's going to happen."

Footballers in those days weren't the multi-millionaires that they are now. Our basic wage was OK, but the bonus payments we received for playing in and winning games made a huge difference. Fergie recognised this and he told me that he was keeping me on the full bonus for three months, reducing to 50% for the following three months and then 25% for the next three. "That will help you, and by that time you'll be back in the first team, so you just concentrate on recovering and getting yourself fit." What an incredible gesture.

I didn't recognise it at the time, and probably very few people would have back then, but he was managing my 'sick leave' and starting the 'return to work' process, a procedure that would have been very rare in any type of business in those days, let alone a football club. And he did it in text book manner, even before the text book had been written. He understood the problem and helped prepare me to deal with it. He, along with the doctors and club physio, set targets towards getting me back to work, and then as time went on, he created opportunities for a phased return (training with the first team before playing in reserve games) prior to getting back onto the pitch with the first team. I've never felt so valued in my life—and this was at a time that could have been the lowest point of my adult life.

Three years later I lifted the European Cup Winners' Cup in Gothenburg when we beat the mighty Real Madrid before going on to win the European Super Cup and claim the tag of greatest team in Europe, if not the world. My return to fitness and ability to play at the top level once again was much more than a victory for medicine. It was made possible by the words and actions of Sir Alex Ferguson. What he did during my time on the sidelines helped me to recover from a devastating injury; I became a vital part of a team that dominated Scottish football, broke the Old Firm (the two Glasgow sides, Rangers and Celtic) stranglehold in Scotland and then went on to achieve those huge European successes.

It's difficult to imagine how I would have felt if I'd realised my career might have been over. It would obviously have been a terrible blow as I was approaching the peak of my career with so much more to play for. Football was my job; this was how I looked after my family, put food on the table and paid the mortgage on our house. But then at least I had achieved something, winning the Scottish league title with a club that wasn't Rangers or Celtic, not something that many people would ever do. It wasn't a bad achievement for a Spammer from Greenock.

CHAPTER 2
Growing Up

I WAS BORN AT Number 4 Chalmers Street, Greenock, on 23 February 1955. We lived on the first floor of the tenement with six other families on the same level, four floors in total. The toilets were outside and we shared them with all the other families on the landing. I was the second youngest of eight children with five older sisters: Ina, Bridgett, Mary, Theresa and Jean. I also had a big brother called Andrew and a younger sister, Susan. I was named John after my dad while Susan was given my mum's name. Incredibly, the flat we lived in only had one bedroom, with a built-in bed on the wall in the living room and a standard bed in the bedroom. Space was so tight that my older sisters would sleep on the floor or the settee. None of this was particularly unusual at the time as this area of Greenock was a typical post-war industrial area housing estate. Many families lived their lives this way and most didn't ever have the opportunity to change things.

There were tenements on every side of us, but we had a great swing park right in the middle where everybody would gather to play. Rough as it was, people looked after each other, so it always felt like a safe area to grow up in. Just down the street and across Port Glasgow Road was the Scott Lithgow Inch Green Dry Dock and the shipyards that stretched for miles on either side, employing thousands of people. Behind Chalmers Street was the railway line that connected Greenock and Gourock, taking passengers the 20 or so miles to Glasgow. Apart from the shipyards we had sugar refineries and textile mills that kept the local people busy and a river, the Clyde, full of ships from all over the world. The yards were incredible places which often saw six, seven or sometimes eight ships of all types being built at the same time, while the dry dock's most famous visitor was the *Queen Elizabeth II*: the Cunard flagship, one of the most iconic cruise liners in the world. The QE2 was built further up the river in Clydebank but fitted out in Greenock before going out on its sea trials.

My dad, Miffy, as he was known, was one of the many thousands of local people who worked in the shipyards. He was a riveter, a dangerous job that involved working with red hot steel. He had to get the timing spot on to get the rivets into the hulls of the ships. Accidents weren't an unusual occurrence in the workplace back then, and my dad was all too aware of the risks. His own father had tragically been killed while working on the railways when he was crushed by two compartments of a goods train.

We moved further up Greenock to Gibshill when I was five. The Gibby, as we called it, was once featured in the *Glasgow Herald* after it had earned the unenviable tag of 'the roughest scheme in Western Europe'. The people there tended to have a tough upbringing, with money being so short that they had the reputation for only ever being able to eat tins of Spam – hence my nickname, Spammer. For us, though, it was just home.

We were really lucky to move, as we managed to secure a new four-bedroom house in Poplar Street. This was absolute luxury to us with all the extra space. We finally had an inside toilet, a living room that wasn't used as a bedroom, a scullery and even a coal bunker. It was a godsend for my mum and dad. My dad soon got to work sorting out the garden, planting fruit and veg, and he even built a shed for storage. Life seemed just about perfect, but tragedy was just around the corner.

Not long after we moved house, my dad fell into the river while fishing with his friends at Pottery Shore next to the gas works. He disappeared below the water. Ten days went by before his body was discovered. Our family had been robbed of its head. He was only 43 and he left behind my mum and eight children aged between 5 and 17. I was just five years old at the time. It's been devastating to have spent such little time with him; I've lived almost my entire life without my dad. I regularly find myself going past Pottery Shore and still wonder why it happened. He should have had a happy and long life with my mum and the family in our new home. I still miss him and wish he had been around to see what we all achieved.

At the age of five I began my education at Ladyburn Primary School in Greenock, where, being the seventh McMaster kid to go there, all the teachers immediately knew who I was. It was a great school, very well run by the tall, bespectacled head teacher, Miss Pollock. We all liked her, but you didn't mess with her—when she said it was Wednesday, it was Wednesday, even if it wasn't! My sisters kept an eye on me, particularly Theresa and Jean, making sure that I behaved and stayed out of trouble. The playground was huge, which allowed the girls to play with their skipping ropes while the boys ran around playing tig and kicking a ball about. The football was great fun but not too serious for me at this point.

Moving up to secondary school a few years later was a big change. Things were tougher and I found that I had to look after myself a bit more, so it was good to have my brother, Andrew, there to watch out for me. I had a great group of pals too and we all stuck together. Every break time meant games of football all around the playground; sometimes four matches were taking place at the same time. These games were important, and at times the teachers would keep an eye on them to identify the best emerging talent. Then, on a Friday, Mr Allan, the school football team coach, would announce who had been picked to play for the school teams at the weekend in the various age groups. Mr Allan was an outstanding teacher who engaged a lot of the older pupils to help him identify the best of the younger players, asking their advice before picking the teams.

This was at a time when teachers were happy to help with the sports teams in their own time, and luckily for me, Mr Allan realised that I had some ability. It wasn't just football that I was decent at either; I always did pretty well at PE in general.

Another teacher, Mr Dunsmore, recognised this and helped me along. He got me into long distance running, with lots of training designed to build up my stamina and endurance. I got an early introduction to that wonderful feeling of being successful when I won the Inverclyde and school's long-distance race at Battery Park in Greenock. That was soon topped when I finished first in the county championships. The Business of Winning started early for me!

Despite the successes that I achieved in running, Mr Allan continually shared his belief that I could do well at football. He made me captain of the teams that I played for, in every year group, and I am eternally grateful to him for his support and encouragement. He was an art teacher, as was his wife, but they both had a great passion for sport. Mrs Allan knew my sisters well, as they played for the netball teams that she ran. People like the Allans were so important back then in getting kids involved in sport. They were invaluable.

They wouldn't have seen much of me in their art classes, though, as that wasn't really my thing. I tried my best with the academic subjects like maths, English and history, but I wasn't really that clever. I did like woodwork and metalwork, though, plus PE, of course. This was pretty much the case for most of my pals too, at least the ones whom I played alongside in the school teams. And most of them would follow the same immediate career path as me, using our practical skills when we'd had enough of school, taking the first opportunity to leave education and go and find work. Of course, in those days, that meant we were still kids really, just 15 years old.

It was easy to find a job in Greenock back then. My brother, Andrew, was a coppersmith in Kincaid's. Founded in 1868, Kincaid's was regarded as the best engine builder not only in the UK but worldwide. They were a large engineering firm who supplied the turbines and engines for ships being built on the Clyde and all over the globe; a truly world class company, like so many others in the area. My brother advised me to put my name down for the Scott Lithgow Training Centre, which I did, and my application was successful. Scott Lithgow was the biggest shipbuilding company around and getting into the training centre was the first step on the road to working in the shipyards. I don't want to overstate it but, on reflection, being immersed into an industry that was at the top of its game must have had a positive impact on me in later life.

The first four weeks were a steep learning curve for me. I was in a group of 10 apprentices; we had four weeks trying the various trades to see which job we were best suited to. I ended up in the plumbing department, which I didn't particularly want to do, but it worked out OK. I became the best apprentice plumber from that 1970/71 group, although I don't remember getting a medal for it!

Each year the training centre supplied approximately 500 apprentices to the local shipping industry. That's how large and vibrant the shipyards were back then. There are now fewer than 500 people employed across all parts of the shipbuilding industry in Inverclyde. It's really sad to see the demise of an industry that was such a key part of the community.

The yard that I was assigned to was called the Cartsburn Yard, down by the Victoria harbour. The plumbers' shop was on its own to the left, next to the small drydock, and then on the other side was the biggest fabrication shed that I have ever seen. It was as long as the main road and joined up with the Cartsdyke Yard, which was also huge. There was a giant basin in the middle of these two shipyards where ships would be fitted out after being launched. The big yards would concentrate on cargo and supply ships, and Cartsburn also developed the capability to build submarines. At any given time there would be about six or seven ships being built at the same time in the larger yards, while the smaller yards would be building ships for the Navy. These smaller yards also built ferries and tug boats for the government. It kept everyone busy; there must have been at least 15,000 local people employed by the yards in those days. What a great era that was! Those yards were right up at the top of the list of the world's great shipbuilders, and it was fantastic that I had the opportunity to work there.

Obviously back in those days there was no question that the yards were totally male dominated. The local area was lucky, though, to have plenty of industrial factories and textile mills around that gave the local women plenty of employment opportunities too. There was the Gourock Ropework, the mills and the textiles industry, along with the sugar houses and many other places of employment. Greenock was a very busy industrial heartland. We had plenty of work available, which by its nature meant that you were well educated, not only in the skill of your trade, but you also learned what was expected of you. The tradesmen who taught you were typically hard-working, decent men but were not backward in offering their opinion of your ability, commitment and behaviour. Given the close-knit nature of families, neighbours and work colleagues, it wouldn't take long for these tradesmen to find out if you had been up to no good outside work and they would deal with you as they saw fit!

That was Greenock and Inverclyde back then; gritty, industrial, tough and challenging. All in all, it was a great environment for me to build what we now refer to as values, something that would go on to play a huge part in my later success in the world of professional football.

With my work development in hand in the Training School and then in the yard, I was able to concentrate my evenings and weekends on my football.

After leaving school and no longer being able to play for my school team, I was scouted for the Port Glasgow Rovers under 16s team. They played in the Paisley and District League, which was the league that most of the boys I had played with or against in school football also ended up in. There were lots of boys from all the local schools playing there, from St Columba's, Greenock High, Gourock High, St Stephens in Port Glasgow and the Mount in Greenock. Although schoolboy signings—or S forms as they were called—existed back then, there wasn't the same sort of mass academy structure that we see nowadays. Most of the decent players from schools would proceed to the juvenile age group leagues, starting at under 16s, then under 18s, before eventually progressing to the under 21s.

All the clubs that we played for had about three teams in each age group who competed in the Paisley and District League. What a structure it was! It produced player after player who climbed the ranks, going on to play in the amateur leagues, for junior teams, and the very best made it to the Holy Grail—professional football in the senior leagues. This structure was replicated throughout Scotland and it produced hundreds of players at all levels. The likes of Davie Provan, another Inverclyde boy, graduated from this structure and went on to play for Kilmarnock, Celtic and he represented Scotland on 10 occasions. Alex McLeish, my future Aberdeen teammate, was a silky midfielder in the juvenile ranks before going on to become one of Scotland's greatest ever defenders. Joe Harper, another Greenock-born player. went on to represent Scotland, Everton, Morton and Aberdeen.

Back then, for many of us, one game a weekend wasn't enough. Before playing for the Rovers on Saturday afternoon, I played for my Boys' Brigade team in the morning. The Boys' Brigade 13th Greenock Company was stationed at the Ladyburn church, right next to my old school. We would go there on a Friday night, and it would be a lot of the usual crowd—me, my older brother Andrew, and a few pals from our classes and others from the streets where we lived. It was something that I absolutely loved, putting on our round hats and the big buckle belt and meeting up at about seven p.m. at the church. The night would start off with marching drills, then we would get stuck into gymnastics, mainly the pommel horse, parallel bars and trampoline. We would finish with a game of football, which was very competitive. I learned a lot from the Boys' Brigade about respect, helping people and mixing with others. I loved every minute of it and looked forward to the games we played on a Saturday morning.

Once the game with the Boys' Brigade was finished, I would head up to Parklea playing fields in Port Glasgow where the Paisley and District League played their matches. There weren't a lot of cars around back then, so if I had money, I could catch the train or the bus out to Parklea, otherwise I would just walk the four miles to get there. This, of course, after playing 90 minutes in the morning and prior to a big game in the afternoon!

Parklea was always a hive of activity. There must have been about 12 pitches, all full of teams of boys of different ages. The dressing rooms and showers were tiny, but we just got on with it—it wasn't like we knew any better. There would be games being played from nine a.m. until three p.m. It was like a conveyor belt of teams! We would wait outside until the sides who had finished playing had cleared out and the dressing rooms were freed up. Then there was the nervous wait to see if you had been picked to play.

When I played with the under 16s, the manager was wee Alex McKenzie and his assistant was big Joe Robb. They were always buzzing and liked a joke, but they constantly wanted to win. I had a full year with them before moving up to the under 18s, where Campbell O'May was the manager with Ian Hemphill as his assistant.

They were good guys who were always pushing me to improve. They looked after me too. Sometimes I didn't get a game for the under 18s, so instead of watching them, I was encouraged to play for the under 21s. I was only 16 at the time, playing with what looked like grown men, some of whom were nearly four years older. It was pretty daunting. At first, I was a bit wary of the physical side of the game, playing with and against these bigger, older guys, but the under 21s manager, Tommy Mooney, and his assistant, Jim Collins, were brilliant with me, constantly letting me know that I was good enough to handle it. I soon grew to love playing with the older players as my fears dissipated. I looked at it as an opportunity to gain experience and to make myself a better footballer. The added bonus was that Tommy and Jim both drove, so after my second game of the day at least I got a lift home!

They were great days, and I loved every minute of it, but my life was about to change forever. The change had been coming for a while, although I hadn't realised it at the time. A local man, John McNab, was a scout for Aberdeen and he had been watching me since I had joined the Rovers. He must have liked what he'd seen, because one day he approached the club and asked them if I could go up to Aberdeen for a two-week trial along with my teammate, Robert Street. Rovers were delighted for us and agreed to let us go. We must have done well, because Aberdeen soon said that they wanted to sign us both.

Before we signed, however, I was invited down to Leicester City for a week's trial with two fellow Greenockians who also played for the Port Rovers—Jim McKimm and Eddie Mayes. Leicester were a team that looked to be on the up at that time, having recently been promoted to the old First Division, the top tier of English football. They had some footballing greats in their ranks like Peter Shilton, Frank Worthington and Alan Birchenall, but although I enjoyed the experience, I was never going to sign for them. By then my mind and heart were firmly set on Aberdeen. I got the impression that the Leicester manager, Jimmy Bloomfield, wasn't too keen on Scottish players anyway, but it was still a good excuse to get away for a week, to see first-class players in action and experience a different football set-up.

When I returned from the Midlands, John McNab and the chief scout of Aberdeen, Bobby Calder, a big name and well-respected scout at the time, came to my mother's house in Gibshill. He introduced himself and asked to speak to me, but I wasn't in. I was out in the streets playing football as usual. Bobby and John, armed with a contract in their pocket, went searching all over the Gibby for me. They were desperate for my signature. I was going to become an Aberdeen player, but they had to find me first! My family and neighbours joined them in the search and they found me eventually, kicking a ball about with my mates. The sense of anticipation was amazing, knowing that this guy had travelled all the way down from Aberdeen with the sole mission of signing me as a professional footballer. I had been playing football for free and now I was going to be paid for doing what I loved.

We got back to the house and went through all the fine detail. Bobby offered me £12 a week and an £80 signing on fee. What a nice shock that was! I was on £4.50 a week at the time as an apprentice plumber—they were offering me almost three times that! My mum and I didn't know what to do at first. We were so shocked that we couldn't speak. Bobby must have thought we weren't sure about accepting, so, not wanting to lose the opportunity to sign me he then said, "I'll tell you what, John, we will make it £16 a week." This was just mind-blowing money for me, and I realised that the wonderful thing was that it would allow me to send some cash down to my mum to help her out, while I'd still have plenty to get on with. At that point I said to Mr Calder that I would be delighted to sign for Aberdeen.

There was, however, a little hint of sadness. I was a Morton fan at the time, and I would have loved to have signed for them but, despite them being my local club, they never approached me. So I ended up joining Aberdeen in February 1972, just before I turned 17.

Formed in 1903, the Dons were a club with a rich history. After winning promotion to the top division two years after their formation, they are one of a handful of clubs who have never been relegated. Although they were competitive, it wasn't until David Halliday became manager in 1937 that Aberdeen began to win trophies—the Scottish Cup in 1947, followed by the league title in 1955 and the League Cup a year later. However, the proceeding years were barren, and by the time I arrived at Pittodrie in 1972, the club had only added one more Scottish Cup to the trophy cabinet. I was joining a club with potential, a sleeping giant!

Robert Street, who was scouted along with me, signed up too, and he travelled up with me on the train. When we arrived at Pittodrie, we were introduced to Mr Jimmy Bonthrone, the Aberdeen manager. He took us into his office one at a time and the first thing he said to me was, "I believe you were an apprentice plumber in the shipyards, John. Do you still want to continue your apprenticeship?"

That wasn't an option for me anymore. I was glad to be out of the shipyards and doing what I really wanted to do. I wanted to give everything I could to make it as a footballer and I told him that. He seemed to like my answer and I liked his response even more! He said, "I see Bobby has offered you £16 a week with an £80 signing on fee." I nodded my confirmation. "Well, I'll tell you what. We will make it £20 a week and a £100 signing on fee." Wow! Now I was on five times what I had been earning. I couldn't believe it! This was the best thing that had ever happened to me in football and it was all thanks to John McNab, the scout who had spotted my talents. My sadness at not being signed by Morton disappeared pretty quickly!

CHAPTER 3
A Family Man

AT THE TIME OF my move to Aberdeen in 1972 I had a steady girlfriend. Katy lived not far from me, in Gibshill's Thomas Muir Street. Back then, at the weekend, my mates and I would get together and get a carry out and have a few drinks in a park or in someone's house if we could. Aged between 16 and 17, we couldn't always bluff our way into pubs, so we had to find other ways of having a drink. Some weekends, though, we would go into the town and try to get into the dancing at the local pubs and clubs. The licensed premises weren't quite as strict then. The local girls would do the same as us, so we would all meet up later on in the evening. We were quite close as a group, and Katy and I liked each other and got on well. We started going out together after a few weeks. She came from a big family, just like me, with three brothers and three sisters—seven kids in total. It was strange because my older sister, Theresa, was a good pal of Katy's older sister, Sadie, so I'm sure it was meant to happen for us.

During that time of growing up we would be working throughout the week and then meet up at the weekend. It was non-stop between the football during the day and drinking, dancing and socialising at night. If we stayed in Gibshill, we would have a game of football on the Saturday and Sunday and then listen to the pop charts on someone's radio to see who was number one that week. It was great—just a normal life for teenagers back then. If we managed to go to someone's house, we would have the radio on as loud as possible while we enjoyed a few drinks. The girls would be dancing and singing too. On Sundays we would all meet up at the shops and have more laughs together. Katy and I were getting serious during that time and I must have fallen in love with her, because we are still together now, 50 years later!

We got engaged when I went up to Aberdeen, I was just 17 years old at the time, Katy was 20, and within two years we were married.

It was the best thing I did, and it helped my football too, as it made me realise that I had to work hard and make a living for me and Katy. Back then it wouldn't have been the done thing for Katy to move to Aberdeen before we were married, so she stayed in Greenock at first, which was hard. I was always desperate to go back and see her at the weekend, and I'm sure this must have been a distraction from my blossoming football career. Once we were married, Katy could move to Aberdeen with me, and that gave me more time to concentrate on my football, as well as the security of having her with me.

Our marriage had been planned for June 1974, but we brought it forward to 21 December 1973. Charlie Ferris, the groundsman at Pittodrie, said he had a flat that was available to rent in an area called Peterculter, but needed to let it out before the end of the year. As he couldn't wait until the middle of the following year, we decided to move fast. I spoke to Katy, and we were pleased to go ahead with an early wedding and picked the Mid Kirk church in Greenock. It seemed a strange time to marry, four days before Christmas, but the opportunity to get the flat was too good to pass up. We spoke to Charlie and agreed to move in as soon as we'd tied the knot.

It seemed like a solid plan, but a couple of weeks later Charlie approached me and said that his wife had rented the flat out to her nephew. The wedding was now booked, so we had to go ahead and get married, even though we no longer had a home to go to! We ended up sharing a flat with Robert Street and his wife, Mary, which meant Katy and I had to sleep on the living room floor. What a great start to married life! To make it worse, it was another one of Charlie's flats that we were living in, which rubbed salt into the wound a little bit!

Fortunately, we were only there for a month, as we managed to get a room at a bed and breakfast for the next four weeks. Then we heard about a room that was available in Constitution Street, just 10 minutes from Aberdeen's stadium. Some of the other players already lived there and were well looked after by the landlady, Mrs Maxwell, or Ma Maxwell as they all called her. She owned the B&B and had always looked after the players at Aberdeen—the likes of Walter McCall, Bobby Glennie and Robert English all stayed there—so we knew what we were getting when we went to see her. She was brilliant, and this settled us down after a tough start to married life together without our own home. Our room had a cooker in it, a fireplace and a television. What a difference that made to us. We had been lucky to have shared Robert's flat, but this was so much better for us. It may not have been superstar luxury yet—I can't imagine Cristiano Ronaldo would have experienced anything similar when he first arrived in Manchester to play for United—but it was good for a young couple from Greenock.

We stayed there for about a year before a flat around the corner came on the market. It was a one-bedroom first floor flat in Summerfield Terrace and was absolutely perfect for us. We managed to cobble the money together and bought it at a cost of £4,300. That was to be our home for the next three years and the place where we started our family. My eldest son, John, was born on 12 July 1976 and then Steven arrived a couple of years later in August 1978. By this time, we had outgrown the flat, so it was time to move again. We found a much bigger place on Sunnyside Road that was more central but still only 20 minutes from the stadium. It was a self-contained flat that had two bedrooms plus a loft space, which was perfect for us. We loved it there and, after a couple of years, in July 1981, son number three, Scott, arrived on the scene.

Our growing family meant that it was soon time for another move and this time, in 1983, we decided to venture out of the city. With my football career now going well, we were able to move to Bridge of Don, into a three-bedroom detached new build. The boys loved it; the area and even their school, Glashieburn Primary. There were also a few of the other players who lived in the same area, like Billy Stark, Peter Weir, Johnny Hewitt, Jim Leighton and the physio, Davie Wylie. We were really settled there and it could have been our home for many, many years, but in 1986 I got an offer from my hometown team, Greenock Morton, to sign for them. This was the club that I had supported when I was growing up and who I had hoped would sign me as a 17-year-old. I had a few other offers—Brechin and Forfar both wanted me to be their player-manager—but I spoke to the Boss and took his advice and went for Morton.

They offered me first team football and also gave me a job as reserve team coach which was very attractive for me. At long last I got to play for Morton and at the same time I could help develop their youth system. It was a win-win situation for me in terms of the football and the job, but of course it meant uprooting the family and moving away from Aberdeen. There were big regrets about that; Katy and I loved Aberdeen, and for the boys it was home—it was their birthplace. As it turned out, they would get an extra year up there, as the oil industry was going through a bad spell at the time and house prices collapsed. Unable to sell our house, I had to stay with my sister, Theresa, and her husband, Eddie Guiller, back in Gibshill for a year, while my family remained in Bridge of Don. It took a full year before our house was sold and then at last we were together again when we moved to Erskine in 1987. We stayed there for 10 years until we came back to Greenock in 1996, to the house that we live in now and where we are very happy and settled. Scott and his partner, Evelynn, made us very proud grandparents when our grandson, Liam, was born on 23 December 2005. That was a special day. The Boss used to accuse me of being too much of a family man—I guess I'm guilty as charged!

CHAPTER 4
Leading The Way

DURING MY EARLY DAYS at Aberdeen, us younger players were given great support and coaching by the highly rated international goalkeeper Bobby Clark. Bobby was a well-educated, clever man and his 17 caps for Scotland fell way short of what I believe he was worth. I'll tell you a funny story about Bobby.

He went to the 1978 World Cup in Argentina along with our club mates Stuart Kennedy and Joe Harper, and Bobby ended up rooming with Stuart. Scotland's preparation for that competition had been very poor, both on and off the park. The hotel that they stayed at wasn't very nice and was in an area with very few facilities or attractions to keep the players occupied. Bobby, though, passed his time reading, always keen to keep his brain stimulated.

After a few days he told Stuart that he needed to send some postcards back home, so the two of them headed down to a little shop close by. The hotel wasn't in a typical tourist resort, so there was only a small selection of cards available, but that was fine for Stuart, as he only wanted one or two. Bobby looked at the remaining pile, about 20 of them, and took the lot. Back in their hotel room, Bobby began to write his postcards. Names and addresses for all 20 recipients were rolling straight off the top of his head, ingrained in the thinking man's memory. The words flowed on the cards, creating a clear picture of the trip that they were on. Nothing could break his rhythm, although Stuart tried his best. Half way through writing the first of his two cards, with the addresses having been copied from a scrap of paper, Stuart looked up from his scribbles and asked, "Bobby, how do you spell mediocre?"

Bobby didn't flinch from his own writing as he reached out his hand and tapped a nearby dictionary a couple of times. "You'll find it in there, son. You'll find it in there."

I was very fortunate that Bobby was one of the senior players who recognised my ability and potential when I was still a youngster. At the time, being encouraged by Bobby to stay behind for additional training seemed straightforward. I would focus on my passing, fitness, all the usual attributes that a professional footballer or athlete would be expected to work on. In hindsight, though, what was just as important with all this was how it helped to build my character. I became not only technically better, but inwardly I was setting good habits and building resilience, standards and so on.

Bobby Clark wasn't the only one involved in doing extra work and willing to help out with the younger players. My fellow Greenockian and top striker, Joe Harper, often spent time sharpening his striking skills, but just as important was his coaching and the work that he did with reserve players who were willing to work with him. Others, such as Davie Robb, also contributed. Davie may not have been such a high-profile player, but what an influence he had on those around him both on and off the park. He also worked with Teddy Scott, the reserve coach, helping him with the second-string players and passing on his knowledge to the younger kids coming through. Davie showed that you did not need to be a star to be a key influencer.

This all went on before the arrival of Billy McNeill and then the Boss himself but only involved a few players and in a very informal way. In reality, the club was not pushing itself hard enough at any level. We were happy to be runners up. You need leadership on the shop floor, not just at the top. Leadership is not a title, it's an attribute and needs to exist at all levels at all times.

I always had a good level of self-belief in my ability, but I was slightly shy. I wasn't the type to push myself forward verbally, I liked to do my talking on the park. I suspect my shyness came somewhat from my family circumstances. As

I've mentioned, my father had tragically died when I was young, so I lived in a predominantly female household consisting of my mother and six sisters. I was always well looked after, but I didn't have the benefit of a father's advice, although my Uncle Andy was always a great support to me. Another guy who was a great help to me growing up was my schoolteacher, Mr Dave Allen. He saw that I had talent and throughout my time at school was always encouraging me and helping to build my confidence.

After Katy and I wed at the tender age of 19, the responsibility I felt of being a family man at a relatively young age contributed greatly to how my career would turn out. When we bought our first flat, I had a mortgage to pay and eventually kids to look after, but I wasn't getting a game during my early days at Aberdeen, so I knew that I had to work hard to get on, to push myself into the team. It was during this time that Teddy Scott was a great support to me. Some of this support was around fitness and technique, and I would do my training with the whole squad and then the extra afternoon sessions with the likes of wee Joe before going home. But Teddy also took the time to talk and listen to me, and that was crucial in driving me forward. What was really great and extremely important was that the discussions were not just about football but also about what was important to me in a wider context.

In spite of all this I was still not getting a game under then manager Jimmy Bonthrone, and I was beginning to feel frustrated and angry inside. Fortunately, I was strong enough, given all the support that I was receiving, that I kept telling myself that I was better than the players who were keeping me out of the team. I was developing a high level of resilience!

However, Jimmy Bonthrone made a decision that started my journey to the top. Positive outcomes, however, don't always appear positive at the time. He loaned me out to Peterhead, who at that time played in the Highland League, a team made up of semi-professional footballers. My teammate, Willie Miller, had been there the year before, and it didn't do him any harm. He played up front for Peterhead, scoring over 20 goals in his solitary season there. It was only on his return to Pittodrie that he was converted into a centre back, where he would go on to become one of the greatest in the club's history, a real 10 out of 10 man every week.

At Peterhead I started to play regular first team football, which built my confidence, technical ability and sharpness in what was a tough league to play in. Great things were happening but, again, with the benefit of hindsight, the most important aspect was that it was building my character. Whilst I was technically superior to most of the players at that level, I was a teenager competing with grown men. Men who were mature, tough and totally committed. Farmers, joiners, welders by day, they had no fear of a youngster and were going to do whatever it took to get the better of me. Those guys, both my teammates and our rivals, taught me a lot about character in a relatively short period of time.

It was an invaluable experience that too many at the top don't fully appreciate, and I include people from all walks of life in that. I had a great season with Peterhead, scoring 13 goals from midfield, a return that delighted my manager. It wasn't an easy time for me, though, as I often left Aberdeen at seven a.m. and didn't return home until nine or ten o'clock at night.

Ironically, I actually scored twice in a game against Aberdeen! We played a testimonial match against the Dons for John Anderson, a Peterhead stalwart, and I put us 2-1 up in the first half of a game that eventually finished 2-2. I'm sure that my performance made a few at Pittodrie sit up and take notice of me. As I said before, I always had belief in my ability, but what I gained from my loan spell was the confidence to speak up, provide support and influence my fellow players, a huge development in my game. I was developing the leadership qualities that Bobby Clark, Joe Harper and others had shown me.

I returned to Aberdeen at the start of the 1974/75 season and played for the reserves—a successful year, as we won the reserve league. I then kicked on and finally made my first team debut. Over the next year I established myself in the first team.

Jimmy Bonthrone left in 1975 and was replaced by Ally MacLeod. I managed to play a few games during MacLeod's first season, but then he signed Jim Shirra to play in midfield and the result was that my first team opportunities were limited. Ally preferred Jim and I barely played for him after that. The future looked bleak for a while, but as usual in football, there's always a twist in the tale. For me that happened in 1977 when MacLeod took over as manager of Scotland's national team and we appointed Celtic legend Billy McNeill as our new manager.

Billy had only had a very short apprenticeship managing Clyde before being lured to Pittodrie, but he was such an iconic leader in Scottish football that it seemed like a no-brainer.

At that time, I was working with the ground maintenance staff during the summer to earn a few extra quid (I told you we weren't that well paid!) and I was the first player to greet my new manager.

The previous season had been difficult for me under Ally MacLeod, spending most of the time in the reserves. I only played five first team games despite having been a regular the season before—clearly Ally didn't fancy me as a player. However, that long spell in the reserves was to work in my favour, despite my frustration and annoyance at the time. John Clark had looked after the Celtic reserves prior to coming to Aberdeen with big Billy. He had seen me play against his team often and recognised what I could bring to the first team. He made sure that Billy knew about my ability, and they soon took me aside and made it clear that they rated me, telling me that I was going to be part of their plans going forward. The ball was now finally in my court; I just had to make sure that I took the opportunity. I felt that the inner strength I had developed from my year at Peterhead, coupled with my natural ability plus the added confidence from a legend like Billy McNeill saying that he rated me, were positioning my career to take a giant step forward. I was now a strong character, had enhanced my technical ability and was keen to become a key part of something special.

I was involved in over 40 games during Billy's first season, scoring a few goals along the way. I'm sure that I'd have broken through anyway, but I've still got a lot to thank John Clark for. He's still a mate to this day.

We only had the one year with Billy, but what a year it was! We reached the Scottish Cup final and finished as runners up in the league. Everything was heading in the right direction for me and the club, and then came another twist in the tale. Billy received a call from Celtic and they asked him to return to Celtic Park to become their new manager, replacing the great Jock Stein. While everyone at the club was disappointed, no one could blame him for returning to his first love, the club where he had lifted the European Cup as captain just 11 years earlier.

The timing, though, couldn't have been worse for me, as I was primed and ready to launch my career forward, having finally established myself in the first team. Billy had signed some very good players who enhanced the team, including the likes of Gordon Strachan, Steve Archibald and Ian Scanlon, so he was leaving behind a strong legacy.

Little did we know that this was the prelude to the next stage, as Alex Ferguson was named as the replacement for Billy. Again, as fate would have it, I happened to be the first player to greet him when he arrived at Pittodrie to start the process of taking Aberdeen FC to the very top. It must have looked like a 1970s version of online stalking, me following all the new bosses around!

It would be an amazing journey for us, and for him it was the next step on a journey that would lead to Manchester United after Aberdeen, his subsequent knighthood and global recognition as one of the greatest managers of all time.

A new manager coming in was always going to be a challenging time for the players. How would we react and what would the relationship between us and such a strong force as the Boss be like? As it turned out, we had a near perfect situation that was very finely balanced, helped by the strong characters within the team, and by that time the team included me. Despite that, though, there was never any doubt that Sir Alex was in charge. However, if the squad had been full of weak characters, I reckon the club would have failed. Similarly, if it had been all about strong characters and their egos, I reckon we would have failed. So why was the mixture of strong characters who were so united in their approach on and off the park so successful? Winning dressing room and training pitch battles was a way of life for us, and that could easily have sparked jealousy and fall outs amongst strong characters with the wrong motivation. For all of us, though, being a strong character in itself was not the goal. The goal was to win everything. This common goal meant that egos never got in the way. Character and ego were necessary means to an end.

Like all things, however, there were unintended consequences, good and bad, or in this case funny and not so funny. Individuals who are strong characters have the tendency to speak openly, which is not always a great thing, as I found out during a game against St Mirren.

We were due to play the Saints at Pittodrie on a Saturday and, as usual, the pre-match ritual was for players to make their own way to the Ferryhill House Hotel for midday—there were no fancy overnight get-togethers in plush hotels in those days! We all gathered in the large downstairs suite that we called the Submarine, where there was plenty of energetic chit chat—the competitiveness had already started. As usual the topics included haircuts, clothes, anything that allowed players to start challenging each other. I've repeated a number of times that with hindsight this behaviour toward each other was a vital component in building our team spirit and resilience; it was constant.

After the Boss and Archie Knox, his assistant, arrived we were given our steak and chips for lunch and then settled down to watch *Saint and Greavsie*, the then popular lunchtime football preview show on television. Not surprisingly, as the programme went on, the mood in the room started to get more and more focused on the game in hand.

It was at this point that Alex McLeish (Big Eck) remembered that he had a message to pass on from my wife Katy. In the now more sombre atmosphere, Alex blurted out in front of everyone, players and staff, "Hey, Spammer," as I was known, "Katy said she has left the pram in the boot of the car." This was the 1980s and the idea of someone being a family man hadn't entirely caught on! The thought of any man pushing a pram was still very much a no-no, so the idea of a top-flight professional footballer doing so was unimaginable. More importantly than that, though, it was a complete distraction from the preparation for the game. We were in a place where there should be no distractions from the outside world. We should have been in our own little bubble preparing for the match ahead.

I looked up at Big Eck, but by then he already knew the impact of his words and he was now looking at the floor, desperately trying to avoid eye contact. The rest of the room, in a synchronised move, turned and looked at me, but worse was to follow. I waited, expecting something furious to come from the Boss, but he said nothing. He didn't flinch, nothing! I was more than a bit surprised, but thankful that I had got away with it. I already knew that I had been selected in the starting line-up, so I was very lucky. There was no dressing down from the Boss and I was still in the team. Anyway, we finished up and headed off to Pittodrie for the game, travelling in our own cars, of course—no plush hotel and no luxury coach with police outriders either!

We arrived at the ground and went through the normal routine; individual pre-match preparation and then the team talk from the Boss. During this time I was still waiting for him to say something about the pram, but nope, nothing. Out we went for the game, and guess what? I had an absolute nightmare first half. I was terrible!

Walking back into the dressing room, I knew that I would be in the firing line and I was right! I had barely sat down when the Boss walked in. His first words were, "Pram! Pram! You and that pram!" I glanced up and managed to catch Alex McLeish's eye. He sat there looking apologetic, hands on his head, but it was too late. The Boss had moved on to other things by this time, but still all this 'pram stuff' had obviously been eating away at him. He worked his way back round to me, still not happy. "Spammer, you know family stuff has to be left outside on a match day," he said. He often told me that I was a good family man, something that would normally have been a nice compliment and something he appreciated in his players. However, the boundaries were crystal clear; match day was work day and all the focus had to be on the game. I had just proved how right he was by my first half performance. And then came the inevitable result of his frustration when I heard the dreaded half-time words. "Spammer, you just sit out the second half." I was subbed and my game was over, all thanks to Big Eck (McLeish) and a pram!

Fortunately, the great thing about the Boss was his ability to deal with something as soon as it happened and then move on. By the time the next game came around I was back in the starting line-up, and the pram was never left in the boot of my car again!

Another more serious incident that occurred in 1980 highlighted the fact that as players, the strong characteristics that we showed on the park remained with us even off it. We were playing against Rangers in the League Cup and I got injured when the Rangers winger, Willie Johnston, stood on my chest, leaving a number of stud marks as an unwanted souvenir. Willie claimed that he had mistaken me for our captain, Willie Miller, with whom he had a longstanding feud. This was an easy mistake to make, obviously, with Willie being a six-foot-tall, dark, curly-haired, moustachioed bear of a player and me being a small, short-haired ginger by comparison! It was a nasty incident and was very painful, but I received treatment on the park and after a short time I had fully recovered, bar a few bruises. Within minutes, however, the story in the press box (and on my Wikipedia page) was that Willie Johnston had stood on my neck and that I had received mouth-to-mouth resuscitation to save my life. No offence to our physio, Roland Arnott, but I'm glad that was unnecessary! On leaving the ground, the press were looking for me straight away, obviously trying to push the story of how life-threatening Johnston's actions had been. However, I corrected them and let them know exactly what had happened and that it was nothing serious. I wasn't going to let them make more out of the incident than there was.

I got on the bus with the rest of the players ready to head back home again, but then the Boss came on and announced that no one was to talk to the press about the incident. He may well have been thinking that this was an opportunity to ramp up the rivalry between us and Rangers even further, and the way the story has grown arms and legs ever since would probably suggest that he was successful. However, I felt I had no choice but to let him know that I had already spoken to them, and he wasn't happy. I could that tell he was about to start off on a rant at me, but before he started, I pointed out there were no instructions given prior to me meeting the press on the way to the bus. I couldn't break rules that didn't exist at the time! "Fair enough, Spammer," the Boss immediately responded. He acknowledged that I was right and that was the end of the matter.

The third example of where a player's strength of personality had an unintended outcome was the famous winner scored by Johnny Hewitt in the European Cup Winners' Cup final against Real Madrid. I'll cover the game in more detail later in the book, but in short, Johnny wasn't having the best of games at the time, and the Boss was clearly very unhappy with him. Johnny realised that he was on the verge of getting a verbal battering from the side of the pitch where Sir Alex stood, so he decided to play as far away from the dugout as possible. As it turned out, Johnny found himself in an unusual position which resulted in him heading home the winner!

The Boss was always in charge, there was never any doubt about that. But he did encourage us to be strong, resilient and never to be afraid to take action or to speak out knowing that if it made sense, he would listen to us and act accordingly. Again, winning was the priority, not big egos.

Becoming a successful football club does not only require a great manager to lead, but the individuals within that team, in that organisation, need to have leadership qualities too. Whilst naturally most of the focus is on the coaching and playing staff, it goes much further than that. As I will cover later, it includes the receptionist, catering staff, gate tellers, people throughout the whole organisation. That's what we had at the club. After we won the European Cup Winners' Cup, the Real Madrid manager, the great Alfredo Di Stéfano, summed it up brilliantly: "Aberdeen have what money can't buy; a soul, a team spirit built in a family tradition." I'm not sure that we even appreciated what we had created, but when we read his words, we realised that he was absolutely correct and this was what made the difference. So it was never just about the 11 players on the park, the extended squad or the manager alone in the dugout. It was the whole club.

CHAPTER 5
The Long Road

GOING BACK TO THE injury that I suffered against Liverpool, I had plenty of time to think about where I had come from and how my life developed following my recovery and during my time out of the game. The nine months recovery plan turned out to be a bit ambitious, but on a scale of nine months to never, the eventual 18 months that it took to recover wasn't that bad! I was in a stookie (a plaster cast) from hip to foot for 12 weeks, then I had a light plaster for the next couple of months. I virtually had to learn to walk again; my muscles had completely wasted away by the time the plaster came off, and my knee wouldn't bend. Our physio, Roland Arnott, worked wonders with me. He helped me to get the leg straight, worked on me every day, and showed me how to self-massage and how to walk with crutches as I started to rebuild.

The physio's room was next to the manager's office, which was a big help, not just for me but for everyone who had a spell out injured. Sir Alex saw everyone who was in there and always had a word or two of support for them, making them feel part of the team. He would be in there every day, talking to the physio and getting an update on the progress of the injured players.

The support from the Boss towards me never wavered during that time. He kept me involved so I felt supported, and he gradually reintroduced me to parts of the workplace when it was feasible to do so. It's incredible how important that was. Some people will make the most of their long-term absences, but the majority would rather be at work. They would be contributing in any way that they could; having interaction with their colleagues, apart from everything else, does wonders for their wellbeing and mental health. I was no different, but the Boss kept me occupied. Obviously, there was a lot of work on the treatment table, and for much of the time I had the legendary Joe Harper beside me, as he was out with a cruciate injury. Two Greenock boys together, so we had plenty to talk about!

The involvement continued and increased as I became more mobile. Sir Alex was driving me on with my rehabilitation, checking my progress and taking a genuine interest in how I was feeling. He established, with his actions, that I was important, not just to the organisation or the football club but to himself as a person as well, which generated a huge amount of respect and goodwill from me. When I came back—and I would come back—I'd run through a brick wall for him.

Once I was able to get about, he would send me to games to get reports on future opponents, identifying how they played and who their danger men were. Apart from providing great information for Aberdeen ahead of our upcoming games, this also set me on the first steps towards my future football career, as I learned lessons with him that I never forgot. Whether it was watching first team games, reserve matches or training sessions, they were great experiences. And some of the greatest experiences were when he would take me with him to visit the youth training camps all over the country.

Sir Alex had his own version of 'Disruptive Technology' designed for the football industry. He created training camps for kids all over the country, changing the historical Aberdeen focus of keeping it local. He wanted to have as much chance as Rangers, Celtic or anyone else to capture the best young talent anywhere in the country, so he knew he had to go where the people were. The camps were set up in Edinburgh, Inverness, Ayr and beyond, and one, Helenvale, was also created in Glasgow, almost at the door of Celtic Park in the East End of the city. He would use his network of ex-players and colleagues to run the camps, but they weren't just satellite camps for others to manage with the hope of finding the next big thing. Sir Alex was hands on, a regular visitor, ensuring that everyone there felt part of the overall club. He also strengthened the local scouting network, a move that was vital in finding the likes of John Hewitt, Neil Simpson, Neale Cooper, Eric Black and Bryan Gunn.

He had this wonderful ability to know all the kids by name and could get down to their level while still maintaining huge respect. On one of my first visits with him to Glasgow he gathered all the under 15s around in a circle in the dressing room and after a brief chat, asked if any of them had a 'burd' (a girlfriend). There were lots of embarrassed faces and nervous giggling, but one slightly cocky youngster stepped forward and said, "Yes, I have."

The Boss replied instantly, "Get rid of her, Billy. They're nothing but trouble!" The kids loved it and felt totally comfortable with him, while learning a very quick lesson in humility at the same time.

The first time that I went to one of the camps with him was during my recovery period, and he asked me to take a training session with the boys. They were just young kids and I had no experience of running a training session, especially for youngsters. When I asked him what I should do in the session, he said, "Just give them what you get, but slow it down a bit to allow for their age." He believed in treating people the same, irrespective of who they were. The boys got lots of ball work, some sprints to push their fitness, practice at keeping possession and worked on their touch before we had a game to finish. They loved every minute of it and so did I. When the boys came to Aberdeen during the school holidays, they would train and mingle with the first team squad and the reserves for much of the time. Everybody had a part to play and everybody was equally valuable in pursuit of the end goal—a belief that stretched throughout the organisation.

We've probably all heard the Boss 'talk the talk', but his actions spoke far louder than even his infamous hairdryer treatment (or the blast furnace as Stuart Kennedy called it)—he 'walked the walk' every day. Working with my business colleagues over the last few years I've been introduced to some formal leadership methodologies, and through that I can see many areas where Fergie displayed the very best qualities. He was an incredible example of what the American business academics James Kouzes and Barry Posner call 'Modeling the Way' in their books. Kouzes and Posner wrote, "Leaders establish principles concerning the way people (constituents, peers, colleagues, and customers alike) should be treated and the way goals should be pursued. They create standards of excellence and then set an example for others to follow." Not only did the Boss know all the kids by name, he knew their parents as well, especially their mothers. He had worked out that the mother would be the one who ultimately decided if the child would be allowed to sign, so she had to be kept sweet.

If they did sign and came to Pittodrie, they would see the Boss routinely do things that were so natural that it was hard not to follow his lead. After an early morning start in the gym, Sir Alex would sit with Bella, who ran the kitchen, making her feel as valuable as the club captain. He would talk with the cleaners who were making the stadium facilities first class, the people who worked on the turnstiles, the physio who was responsible for clearing up the injury list, George the bus driver—everyone who was part of the organisation. And they were all made to feel equally important. And they were, of course. Their jobs all contributed to the end result of winning football matches.

People like Bella became integral to the running of the organisation. More than a tea lady, she was also a landlady, providing accommodation for some of the younger players with a vital role in keeping their attitudes right as well as their diets! George, meanwhile, seemed to be everywhere, buying in entirely to the goals of the club. One minute George would be shifting hampers full of training kit on his own, helping us to get organised for a match or training, next he would be sitting alongside the Boss in the dressing room, still wearing his trusty chauffeur's bunnet (flat cap)!

Sir Alex demonstrated his recognition of the importance that he placed on every individual within the organisation brilliantly during his early days at the club. When we won the league in 1979/80—less than two years after he became manager—for only the second time in the club's history, and 25 years after the first title, the Boss organised a team photo to mark the occasion. It was something for future generations to see and celebrate. The league win was a huge achievement for the whole of Aberdeen and the surrounding areas and was virtually guaranteed with a sensational 5-0 victory over Hibs at Easter Road. Hibs could have been dangerous that day, as they had already been relegated and the pressure was off, but when Steve Archibald and Andy Watson scored in the first half, the belief and the confidence just started oozing out of us. A double by Ian Scanlon and one from Mark McGhee confirmed the stroll. We weren't technically champions on that day—we would need a defeat to Partick Thistle and a massive goal difference swing to deny us—but we knew that we wouldn't be denied!

Back at Pittodrie, with the league championship won, the Boss gathered the whole team in the Dick Donald Stand for the commemorative photograph. And when I say the whole team, I mean everyone; first team, reserves, coaching staff, ground staff, catering people, directors, youth team players, Bella and George—the lot! Everyone had contributed to our success, so everyone celebrated the success. Sir Alex made sure that everyone's contribution was recognised.

Businesses for many years have loved quoting the favourite traditional sayings, like "there's no 'I' in TEAM" and "we have an open-door policy", but how many actually create the environment to allow people throughout the workforce to feel part of, and comfortable with, that environment? Take that idea to the very top and think of the time Donald Trump told reporters that they couldn't challenge him because he was the president while simultaneously telling them that they were terrible at their job because they didn't agree with him. It's an extreme example, but look at the turnover of staff he has had. That is an obvious sign of an uncomfortable work environment.

Making people feel good at their workplace, creating a psychologically safe environment, is vital to get the best out of them. That doesn't mean that you drop the demands on your staff; in fact, it's quite the opposite. You will get greater buy-in to what you are trying to achieve by creating an opportunity for people to express themselves and for everybody to have the chance to step up and show their leadership qualities. To get this, though, you need to routinely demonstrate that everyone is important. Fergie showed that a leader who took the time to talk to his people, involved them in all aspects of the club and recognised their contributions was absolutely vital to making this happen. His results certainly suggest that it worked!

CHAPTER 6
More Than Just The Boss

I'M SURE NO ONE will need to read this book to realise that, wherever Sir Alex was working, there was never any doubt who was 'the Boss'. That seemed to extend beyond his remit, even his football club sometimes, as various members of the press would no doubt confirm—he often kept them in check with a simple look that they knew meant not to go down a certain line of questioning!

The Boss himself has stated that a key attribute in being the boss or the leader is to never cede control. It might come as a surprise that, despite this belief, Sir Alex was very open and responsive to feedback and advice. However, it was always clear that he would be the one to make the final decision and he was accountable for every decision that he made.

Looking back now with the added experience that I have gained by thinking about and analysing those days, it has become clear that he was much more than 'the Boss', albeit one of the most famous and successful ones of all time. It wasn't the title that he took, it was absolutely the job that he did and the man that he was. To this day, my colleagues and many of my former teammates still refer to him as the Boss. In fact, even some of the legends of the game still call him Boss. I loved the bit at the end of the Euro 2016 Championships when Portugal had just won their first major trophy. As Cristiano Ronaldo was walking down the steps after collecting his winner's medal Sir Alex shouted to him from within the crowd. Ronaldo, at that time a Real Madrid player who had last played for Fergie seven years earlier, looked around for a couple of seconds until he saw him and shouted, "Boss!" before pushing his way through the crowd to enthusiastically hug his mentor.

For the last few years I've been developing my knowledge about how the Boss achieved what he did by thinking about many of the stories from my time working with him at Aberdeen. This has allowed me to tell my story to audiences that were looking to get a deeper understanding of what made Sir Alex so successful. While reflecting, my own understanding has developed even further and I have learnt the full range and effectiveness of his methods and style—or maybe that should be styles! The audiences that I've worked with have covered a huge range of people and sectors, including MBA graduates and staff at one of the world's top 100 global MBA schools, professional PDP (Personal Development Plan) courses for legal professionals, senior operatives in the oil industry, a worldwide Association of International Accountants and many more of that ilk. While the vast majority obviously knew who Sir Alex was, they were not, on the whole, particularly interested in football. The most common question that I was asked at these events was, "What leadership style and techniques did he adopt to become the best in the world and a serial winner?" There's no single answer to that question, but some of the stories from our time at Aberdeen help to show just how he went about his business.

He set the scene for how people should be treated from the day he arrived by the way he dealt with everyone. From the very beginning he treated everyone associated with Aberdeen FC with respect, and I mean everyone, from ground staff to youth team members, from the board of directors to first team players—everyone! The league winners' photograph with everyone in it was quite a public display of this, but it was a natural, routine, daily occurrence for him to be close to all the staff. It started first thing in the morning. He would arrive long before any of the playing staff and, after a visit to the gym, he would have an early morning cup of tea and chat with the ground staff. A lot of these conversations would be general chit chat about what was going on, the talk on the street, how their families were doing, what was in the news and so on—standard conversations that would break down barriers and open up opportunities for serious 'work' discussions. And there was nothing false in all of this; it was how Fergie believed that he should treat people.

This was key to building a rapport and trust with the staff, which allowed everyone to feel comfortable, be frank about maintaining high standards and work towards a common goal. Building this level of trust enabled issues to be addressed and dealt with in a positive manner and ensured that the standards that the ground staff were responsible for were being met and, importantly, were supported by all at the club; maintenance and upkeep of the pitch, dressing rooms, terracing and stands, strips, equipment, catering, front office—every aspect of the club.

The environment in which the conversations took place was never a formal 'stand by your bunk' inspection type, but rather an open and frank two-way conversation. The ground staff felt safe in their ability to provide feedback to Sir Alex about where standards were not being respected. If dressing rooms were not left tidy, he would hear all about it, and we knew when he'd heard about it! That was enough of an incentive for most of us to develop good habits and, in reality, the success of this was measured by how infrequently any action was needed. Much of this was also down to the work and support of coach and Aberdeen legend Teddy Scott. Teddy would demand that all players show respect to everyone at the club. He would require that no matter the game or result, when you removed your strip, you did so in a certain way that would make the job of laundering it easier and more productive. It was always about maintaining standards and developing good habits, and that meant off the pitch as well as on it. Once standards are set, it becomes very easy to spot when they start to slip, and action can then be taken to address it.

One of my colleagues recalls the legendary rock and roll story about the band Van Halen, who, as part of their signed agreement for playing a concert, stipulated that they wanted a bowl of M&Ms with all the brown ones removed. This was always assumed to be 'rock star diva' type behaviour until a few years later when they explained all in an interview. When they turned up at a venue, they checked the bowl and if that job was done correctly, they could assume that the rest of their requirements would have been met as well. These were far more important; the number of power supplies, sockets, lengths of cables, position of lighting and so on—all vital ingredients for a successful gig. The M&Ms were just an easy way to see whether standards had been met.

High standards and good habits were always promoted by Teddy, and he instilled those within the youth and reserve players that he coached. As he often said, "You try to teach the youngsters good habits as well as skills and hope that they will still be around in the future when the club can reap the rewards."

Teddy was invaluable to the club. He had many tasks—coach, kit man, confidant, and even the bus driver at times. His contribution and value to the football club was summed up before one away game. Teddy had packed the wrong shorts for the team. Sir Alex wasn't pleased and, in his exasperation, blurted out that he should sack Teddy. Gordon Strachan turned to Fergie and told him that before sacking Teddy he would need to find the ten people who were going to replace him!

Teddy seemed to literally do everything. He was also the original 'Opta stats' man, keeping a record of every player's statistics in reserve games; goals, assists and so on. This provided evidence to the Boss when Teddy suggested that certain players were ready to move up to the first team. He was well ahead of his time and I learned so much from him.

Despite Fergie's exasperation about the time that he brought the wrong shorts to a game, he valued Teddy very highly. He knew Teddy would let him know everything that was going on around the club with the players and staff, something the Boss liked to know all about. He developed an incredible network of people around him who became his eyes and ears, all designed to stop us getting up to mischief to the detriment of the team, and to ourselves probably. Neale Cooper was one player who was caught out by Fergie's surveillance squad when he was hauled in to see the Boss first thing one Monday morning. "What were you doing going to a party in Union Street on Friday night?" Fergie asked.

Neale had been seen going into a city centre flat at about ten o'clock in the evening and, of course, the Boss had heard about it. The explanation, though, was completely innocent, as the 19-year-old Cooper explained, "I wasn't going to a party, I was going to my bed. That's my flat—I just bought it."

The Boss, true to form, went straight back at him. "Nineteen years old and staying in a flat in the city centre? What are you thinking? Sell the flat and get back to your mother's, she'll look after you properly!"

As always, there was method in Fergie's apparent madness; it wasn't just a boss imposing his will on a young employee. He saw the risks for the young man, a celebrity in the city, being too close to the temptations of the city centre nightlife. Many a budding footballing career has been lost when the player has given in to these temptations, and Sir Alex made sure that it wouldn't happen to Tattie, as we called Neale. Cooper would go on to become one of our great players, a legend at the football club, fully justifying the Boss's intervention in his living arrangements!

Teddy was aware of every aspect within the football club, including the financial side. Obviously, our kit was a vital part of doing our job properly, but Teddy wouldn't allow any waste. When I was still young, and probably a little naïve, I remember going to see Teddy looking for some new boots. Teddy looked at the ones I had and asked what was wrong with them. "There's a hole in the left one, Teddy. I need a new pair." Obviously, as a left-footed player, the right boot was perfect due to a lack of use!

Teddy looked at it and said, "Aye right enough, but you know how uncomfortable new boots are, Spammer. And all that fuss with Vaseline and soaking them and so on." The boots in those days were as tough as the streets we grew up on, so I got what he was saying. "Leave them with me, son, and I'll get them mended for you!" He was probably right, but he was also watching his budget, making sure that not a penny was wasted.

He was a guy who had a fantastic way with people. On a Friday before a game, Teddy was responsible for organising the pre-match meals for the players. He would get us all together after training, maybe 18 of us depending on who was fit, and go around individually to see what we wanted to eat later. At that time we only carried a match day squad of 14—11 starters, 2 subs, and 1 spare player for emergencies—so at least 4 of us would miss out. This was when we found out if we were likely to be playing or not, or at least in the squad. Terry would call out, "Spammer, steak or fish? Blackie, steak or fish? Simmie, you can have chips, you're coming with me to the reserve game!" It was hard to get angry when you found out you'd been dropped in such a fashion—and there was the bonus of getting chips!

As you can tell, by the time playing staff had arrived for daily training sessions, the issue of standards and excellence would have already been discussed and each day was being reinforced and institutionalised into all parts of the club. With hindsight I now realise that one probably unplanned but hugely positive outcome was that this expectation of excellence and high standards was now taking place directly between the ground staff and playing staff. Conversations between us were frank, constructive and a safe thing to do. So, from what might seem a rather innocuous early morning nice chat, what was really happening was Sir Alex was showing everyone how he wanted the club to behave as they pursued their goals and objectives – trophies in our case. Indeed, I honestly believe that this was one of the key elements in our success.

Of course, winning was the ultimate goal. He didn't immediately say that we were going to win a European trophy—or two, as we actually did—but he did set out the vision that we would win one trophy first, then two, then three, etc., which we duly did. Of course these goals could by definition only be achieved in the months and years ahead. What do you do to add that winning mentality right now? His answer was simple: "You are going to win at

EVERYTHING, literally EVERYTHING." That included the obvious training activities like sprints, exercises, small-sided games, full 11 aside games, etc. Even that was not enough, as it was not everything, so what might look petty became a symptom of this winning mentality. Playing snooker wasn't recreational, it became a competition. Playing cards wasn't recreational, it became a competition. No matter what we did, we had to win.

Football, snooker and cards are probably obvious examples of the games that footballers like us would have played where we battled for those victories. Cricket, though, would maybe not be high on the list of sports to be played by your standard Scottish footballers, except Andy Goram, who represented Scotland at both cricket and football. However, a game of cricket embodied this winning mentality that had become instilled within the club. Sir Alex had organised a pre-season training camp at the world famous Gordonstoun School. Gordonstoun is about 70 miles north of Aberdeen and is most famous for boasting Prince Philip, the Duke of Edinburgh, and his son, King Charles, as past pupils.

While we were there the Australian and English cricket teams were locked in a battle for the famous Ashes. Sir Alex decided to take a fun break from training to allow the players some relaxation time. We borrowed some cricket equipment and donned the full kits, jumpers and white trousers, and took to the field. First in to bat was Sir Alex, accompanied by centre back Willie Miller. Jim Leighton, our goalkeeper, was the first to bowl and was bowling to the Boss. At this point the rest of us in the batting team were in the pavilion creating some noise and atmosphere by chanting and banging empty tin cans together, very much in the style of the West Indies cricket team supporters. We were having a great time and it became even funnier when we noticed that the Boss was holding the bat back to front! Big Leighton started his run up, bowled, the Boss took a swipe and was immediately caught out. Despite us on the sidelines being on Fergie's team, there was uproar as we cheered him getting out so quickly. However, the quick-thinking Stuart Kennedy intervened to suggest that it was just a trial run. Stuart anticipated that if the Boss was out, this fun break was not going to last very long!

As Sir Alex retained his place in front of the stumps, Stuart's fears were confirmed.

Jim Leighton bowled again. This time the Boss made a poor connection but decided to run anyway. At the opposite end Willie Miller realised that it was going to be tight and decided to stay where he was and shouted to the Boss not to run and to return to his wicket instead. In the confusion the Boss was run out, the wickets smashed, and appeals and cheers rang around the ground. We were all going crazy again at our man being out. He started remonstrating with Willie and then decided to argue that this was just another trial run. This time, though, nobody was having it, and everyone, including his own team, started chanting, "Out, out, out, out." With his winning mentality obviously badly bruised, Sir Alex decided he'd had enough of this recreational stuff, tore up the stumps, walked off the pitch and announced to everyone that the cricket match was finished. We were sent back to training instead! At the time we obviously saw this purely as the Boss being a bad loser, and, of course, that was exactly the point. His and our instincts were ingrained to be winners. Was he a bad loser? Absolutely. There was no place for a *good* loser. That was a trait that we saw time and time again, and at times it cost players their place at the football club.

Gordonstoun was a great laugh and a fantastic bonding experience. You really had to buy in to the 'win at everything' mentality to survive; every day was a battle of wits. It looked like that trip was Neil Simpson's first trip away from home. He got ready for bed on the first night in the dormitory and was wearing the most horrendous pair of pyjamas that we had ever seen. He got an absolute roasting from the boys to the point where he didn't want anyone else to see them. Unfortunately for him, someone got hold of them the next day. As we walked out of the accommodation building to go and train, a light breeze was rustling the flag on the flagpole, except it wasn't a flag—it was Simmie's pyjamas, flying high above the grounds! Neil wasn't getting out of that one without a red face, but I think a few of us ended up with black and blue legs as he took his revenge on the training ground—he was hard as nails!

That was all part of rising to the challenge; take it on the chin and come back fighting, stronger than before. If you couldn't do that, you couldn't handle the really tough, competitive side of the game at the very highest level. Many a player passed through the door at Pittodrie—and every other club, I'm sure—who was loaded with talent but fell short on their desire to cope with absolutely anything that could be thrown at them. I still look at footballers today and think, *he can play, but he looks like he sleeps with the light on!* That sort of player will never hit the heady heights, which is a shame, but attitude in work is vital. In football that means that nothing and no one will stand in the way of the team winning. In business you might want to modify that a little bit, but you need that desire from the whole team to believe in your abilities and to be prepared to push for the very best outcomes for the team—there's no room for second place.

Of course, whilst Sir Alex was going about instilling a change in mentality, day in, day out, he was also looking towards the future and identifying what else needed to change going forward. He quite clearly had a vision and we were all setting out on this remarkable journey with him.

The Boss realised that the players and staff were only part of what Aberdeen FC was. If we were going on a journey, it was important that we took the fans with us. Aberdeen was said to have the largest catchment area of any football club in the country, and the Boss saw the opportunity that this presented.

He saw a huge untapped supporter base in the north east of Scotland. The players bought into this too. We were beginning to realise that we were becoming part of something big, but to succeed we needed to be more than just very good footballers. Sir Alex set out to galvanise the support throughout the region. He ensured that all the players attended as many supporter functions as possible. Connecting with the fans, wherever they were, drove a massive increase in the number of supporters' clubs. Over a period of a couple of years we built the number of clubs from maybe four or five to more than fifty. Again, looking back, this brought more than just matchday revenue; just as importantly it gave the players an added sense of purpose and duty—a responsibility to the fans. All these seemingly little things added together to make a difference and pushed us on. It's something that I still love to this day, the opportunity to meet the fans and talk about the team. It's such a great buzz to get that feeling of affection that the fans had, and still have, for the club and its players.

Change, of course, always carries risk and is often one of the most feared and resisted elements in the workplace. A football dressing room is no different, and Fergie had faced some challenges there too.

Looking to the future of the playing side, Sir Alex knew that he'd have to make some difficult decisions as he looked to take us to the very top. There were some well-established players who for various reasons would need to be replaced. Some of these would be because he wanted the changes to be made, others were a recognition of what happens in football—people move on to what they think is a better opportunity for them. However, Sir Alex was always looking ahead and made sure that suitable replacements were identified before players moved on. We all knew that Steve Archibald was destined for bigger things; he would move on to Tottenham Hotspur before signing for Spanish giants Barcelona, but he was going nowhere until his replacement was ready. He got not one, but two great replacements in Eric Black and John Hewitt, both developed in the youth team, once again reaffirming the Boss's belief in the system.

Other players would need to move on, but not necessarily because they wanted to go. Obviously, there were the players that the Boss didn't think were quite good enough for Aberdeen, but there were also good players who the Boss thought could be causing a distraction and were not on board with what he wanted to achieve. Nothing could get in the way of creating the highest of high-performing teams that he had set us on the road to becoming.

Despite the frequent temptations to change faces, it was very clear that he did not allow personality clashes to jeopardise the immediate results of the team. He recognised that to achieve his vision, he needed to keep building the credibility and reputation of the team as winners. Despite his incredibly strong personality, he did not let any clashes override the good of the club. Businesses, just like football, often suffer from the 'new boss' effect, where a strong-willed leader decides to quickly make their mark by throwing their weight around and making wide-scale changes. More often than not, even if there is an early bounce, such drastic changes disrupt the good parts of the business, throwing the baby out with the bathwater, and things soon deteriorate. Usually, of course, at this point, the leader moves on, quoting his early successes despite the longer-term failings, and the cycle starts again.

There are many examples where the incoming boss can have a negative effect on results by making changes just for the sake of them. A good article to have a look at is "Can A Narcissistic CEO Destroy Their Company?" by Naz Beheshti, Forbes, from 19 October 2018. Although written for business, it mirrors what has already been said.

Sir Alex may also have had a helping hand in avoiding this mistake in an early conversation with the chairman, Mr Donald. Not long after arriving at Aberdeen, he asked to see the chairman. Mr Donald was a great guy; he ran the club well, relying on having good people to make the best decisions to move it forward. He looked after the financial side of matters very frugally. He was the sort of person who would go around switching off the lights in the rooms that weren't being used, setting a great example to everyone.

One day, early in Sir Alex's tenure, Mr Donald invited him into the boardroom and asked him what he wanted. Sir Alex told him, "I need to sign a defender and a winger, Chairman." Mr Donald nodded encouragingly, but then took Fergie over to that season's squad photograph.

"Look at that, Alex," he said. "There are about 40 players

in that photograph. Go work with them and come back and see me in six months if you still think you need some players." The Boss took the hint and went and developed the players in the squad. He didn't need to go back to see the chairman six months later.

This advice stayed with Fergie throughout his career. He recognised that while looking for ready-made replacements was a well-established method within the football world, it was expensive in terms of time and transfer fees, and, more importantly, adapting new players to the culture and mentality required at Aberdeen FC could be difficult.

So something had to change; he needed to improve an established youth system to make sure that there was a conveyor belt of talent waiting in the wings. They would come through the system with the same mental approach as the first team and would be ready to make the step up without too much further education being required. As part of that process, he got the youth players and reserves training with the first team. They were all treated the same as the first team and so they began to think like the first team. For the most talented, they soon became part of the first team. They knew that they could be called upon at any time to play for the first 11. And as much as Teddy Scott was routinely left to look after the reserve games, the Boss took a direct interest in them and he would often show up at their matches. When someone was ready to make the step up, Fergie already knew all about them and had seen them in action. Next time you read about Manchester United's famed Class of '92, you'll realise just where that success story started.

While he was building and developing the club for the future, he always maintained that personal caring touch, a side of him that many people don't realise existed. He applied that to the established players as well as the kids, not to mention every single member of staff that worked at the club.

Sometimes he moved in mysterious ways. He obviously had a public image of being temperamental, a bit of a firebrand, and of course he had that within him. We've all got these pictures in our heads of him red faced and ready to burst, hair standing up on end and his eyes popping out, waiting to savage a referee or an opposing manager. Sometimes, though, you had to look beyond that to see what he was really doing and why he was doing it.

Usually when he was acting like this he was really looking after us, the players, and our careers, and of course that would have an impact upon the club. We were mostly young men, many of us away from home for the first time, with all the new opportunities that came with having a little bit of money and a little bit of fame. There were opportunities for us to do things that we had never had the chance to do before and some new experiences for us to try.

For some that would have been buying nice new clothes, for others it meant taking up golf. Big Doug Rougvie, though, decided to get a motorbike! A brand spanking new bike! When he turned up for training on the bike for the first time, he was spotted driving into the car park by the more experienced Stuart Kennedy.

Kennedy got a hold of Doug before he got to the dressing room and said, "The Boss will go bananas if he sees you on a motorbike!" Stuart suggested that he put it at the back of the car park and leave it there so the Boss wouldn't see it.

Big Dougie appreciated it and said, "You're right, that's a great shout, thanks," and headed straight back out to shift the bike. However, while he was out moving it, Kennedy spotted the Boss in his office, stuck his head through the door and asked if he knew how big Doug had got in to work today. The Boss twigged that something was going on, so when Rougvie was walking back in towards the dressing room five minutes later, he didn't make it past the office.

"Rougvie—in here!" was the shout from the Boss. "How did you get here today?"

"Eh, my wife, Brenda, dropped me off," replied Doug, having taken the hint from Stuart that the bike may not have been a great idea.

The Boss's hair stood up on end a little bit more. "Rougvie, I'm going to ask you again," he said. "How did you get here?"

"I came in on my new motorbike," came Doug's honest reply.

Sir Alex couldn't believe what he had heard. "A motorbike?" he exclaimed in complete astonishment. "What are you thinking about? You'll break a leg on that. Get rid of it and take the bus from now on!"

Once again, just like with Neil Simpson and his flat, it seemed like a classic hot-headed and unreasonable boss at work, but deep down he was protecting Doug, and with it, the team as well. Not that big Doug saw it that way at the time—he just wanted to ride his bike. But the Boss knew the dangers of a young lad on a motorbike where one fall could break a leg, end his career and disrupt the team at the same time. Fergie couldn't and wouldn't let that happen.

The Boss made him get rid of it and he did that straight away, but not before he got pelters in the dressing room for bringing it to work that day. By the time that he joined us after his visit to see the Boss, we were all waiting to hear what had happened, because Kennedy had told us all about how he had set it up. Big Doug walked in and we asked him innocently what the gaffer had wanted with him. The big man was a bit annoyed and let us know about the bike and how someone had grassed him up to the Boss. Although Stuart had really just been looking after Doug, he decided to play it safe and suggested that Charlie Ferris, the groundsman, might have been responsible, as he had been around the car park area earlier! He was Big Doug after all; better safe than sorry!

I also find it interesting, thinking back to this story, that the Boss's caring side, even in its mysterious guise like this, did rub off on the players. Stuart hadn't just grassed Doug up to the Boss for a laugh, although that was an added bonus. He understood the risks as well and wanted his teammate to avoid them. This was part of what Sir Alex had created—a team that all pulled together with a common purpose.

So, going back to the earlier point in this chapter as to the most common question I am asked, namely what is Sir Alex's leadership style? This is something I discuss with my colleagues regularly and now have some familiarity with the

Chalmers Street, as rough as it was, always felt like a safe place to grow up. We all gathered in this swing park to play.

In my late teens during the early days under Jimmy Bonthrone.

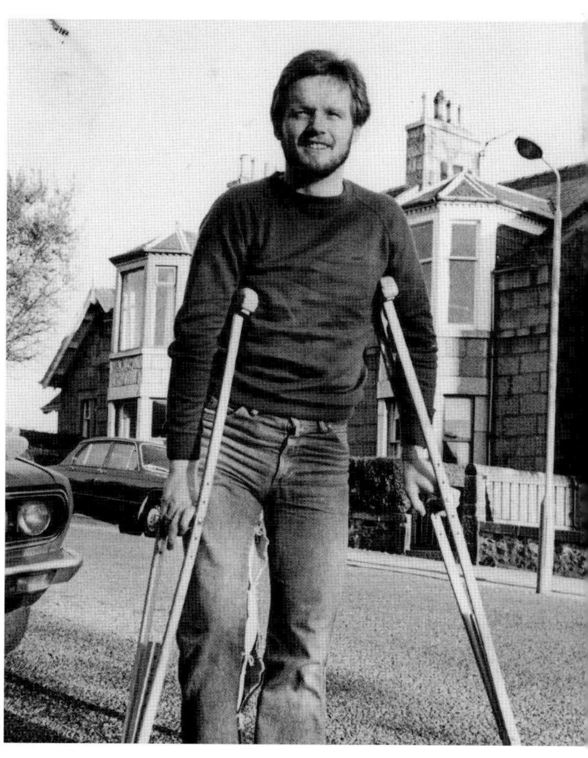

Hobbling down Sunnyside Road during the long journey to recovery.

Roland Arnott, sitting in the dugout, was an absolutely vital factor in me getting back to playing football.

Putting in the hard work at Seton Park.

Everything changed when the Boss arrived at Pittodrie in 1978.

An early game in the 1978 League Cup against Meadowbank Thistle, en route to the final.

The Boss regularly mucked in on the training pitch.

ABERDEEN FOOTBALL CLUB

AFC

Scottish League Champions
1979-1980
Celebration Dinner
on the occasion of winning the
Scottish League Championship 1979-1980

DINNER MENU

Ogen Melon & Prawns Marie Rose

Consomme Petite Marmite

Roast Sirloin of Aberdeen Angus Beef "Pittodrie"
French Beans Nicoise - Creamed Baby Onions
New Potatoes - Roast Potatoes - Yorkshire Pudding

Baked Souffle "Fly the Flag"

Coffee & After 8's

The Directors extend to the Management, Players & Staff many congratulations & every best wish for next season.

Queens Hotel, Aberdeen · Sunday 11 May 1980

Signatures

Just two years after Ferguson's arrival we were champions!

We won the Scottish Cup in 1983 for the second time in a row.

The Boss joined us to celebrate the cup success with the fans back at Pittodrie

Does my head look big in this? You bet it does!

The 'Gothenburg Greats' celebrating with the European Cup Winners' Cup. We'd just beaten Real Madrid in the final.

The Boss and his long-time assistant Archie Knox celebrate our European success.

The European Cup Winners' Cup was
Sir Alex's first European trophy.
It wouldn't be his last.

Celebrating with the fans when we arrived back at Dyce airport. Nice matching hairstyles!

We beat Hamburg over two legs in December 1983 to win the European Super Cup. At that time, Aberdeen were arguably the best club side in Europe.

Lining up take a free kick against Dundee United in 1984.

After an easier training session on a Friday, trying to get my head round the information on the opposition and my role.

Posing for the annual photo call during pre-season at Pittodrie.

various technical terms that they use such as transactional, transformational, democratic, autocratic, laissez-faire (I know it's definitely not that one!) and so on. I think it is safe to say that we have come to the conclusion that there isn't one of these terms that fits, but rather the answer to the question is that his leadership style is that of a winner who cares for all his people.

CHAPTER 7

No Prizes For Coming Second

THE CARING SIDE OF the Boss obviously came to the fore following that European cup game against Liverpool where I was so badly injured. That match, which should have been the most important of my career at that point, went so badly wrong, but the subsequent support that I received from Sir Alex and everybody at Pittodrie Stadium helped to set me up for what would still be a great career. Things clearly got better in the years that followed that horrendous incident, culminating in lifting the European Cup Winners' Cup on 11 May 1983. And it shouldn't be forgotten that we went on to win the European Super Cup that year after beating SV Hamburg. On that night we were crowned arguably the best club team in the world!

Before Sir Alex arrived at Aberdeen to become our manager, there was a mentality within the whole set-up that we were all quite happy to be legends by finishing as runners up in the league and reaching two cup semi-finals. In some ways this view was shared by the supporters. I personally think that at that time Aberdeen FC would have been viewed as a club that did enough to get by. But getting by wasn't good enough for Sir Alex. He set about taking this sleeping giant of a club forward and turned it into a global, world class football team.

There was no apparent drive for success, and Aberdeen Football Club, as with most other teams within Scottish football at that time, were under the spell of the two Glasgow giants, Celtic and Rangers, who had dominated the game in Scotland for many years.

In the Boss's first year in charge, we did what we did

every so often and reached the 1979 League Cup final, only to lose to Rangers. After the game we travelled to Perth for the post-match runners up meal that the club laid on for us. For some it seemed like a bit of a celebration, despite us losing the game, and the chance to get our hands on a trophy. Beers were being knocked back, cigars were smoked and many of the players were joking and carrying on as if this was a celebration of achievement. It must have looked as if we had won the trophy, not that we were the losers.

With the Boss's desire to never be second best, he noted all this and realised that there were players who perhaps lacked the winning attitude which he needed us to have to be part of an emerging, successful team. He didn't like what he saw and wanted to change the mentality within to one of being a club in the business of winning. He also knew that it would be a long process but, understandably, he didn't realise how quick the recovery process would be. In fact, we won the league the very next season!

At that point, though, after losing the cup final, Aberdeen Football Club was badly in need of a change in culture throughout the playing staff that would help to achieve our vision.

I am not saying that there is no space for relaxation and fun; of course there is, but the culture at the time was that we accepted being second best, and Sir Alex on that night in Perth recognised the need for change. There are no prizes for coming second, and the fun and enjoyment would come from being winners.

I went from two managers who didn't really have that aggression or the belief that they would be successful, managers who were happy just getting to finals, to the likes of Billy McNeill and then Fergie who just wanted to win trophies. Both were driven in everything they did. Obviously, we didn't win every game or every trophy we competed for, but when we didn't win, the Boss would say what he had to say in the 10 or 15 minutes after the game and nothing else was said. The Boss would at that point criticise quickly, put the comments to bed and then get on with making the necessary improvements on the training pitch. He was obviously a big believer in the much-used quotation usually attributed to Stan Matwijiw of the Toronto Maple Leaf ice hockey team, “Don’t let the highs get too high, or the lows get too low.” It’s a phrase that works just as well in business as it does in sport.

It was a lesson that I almost forgot when I finally returned to pre-season training after my year of hell following my knee injury. I was always in the top six at the cross country runs and the sprints; those lessons I had learned in my younger days had driven me to that, where hard work and dedication overcame a lack of natural speed. However, back at training with all my injuries finally cleared up in 1981, I expected to be back in my rightful place in the lead of the training runs. The first couple were disasters and I was nowhere near the front. I thought to myself, *that’s it, it’s over, I can’t do this anymore.* I went to see the Boss, the guy who had been there for me every step of the way, and I told him that I thought I was finished. I didn’t think I would get back to the standards I had set before and I thought I needed to quit the game. Sir Alex sat me down and asked what was making me think this way. “My training is terrible. Even Willie Miller is beating me at the cross country,” I said. Willie was a notoriously bad trainer, one of the few who could afford to be because he was always so good on the pitch.

Fergie looked at me, slightly amazed, and set me straight: “Spammer, you’ve been out for over a year. You need time and you’ll get time. Couple of weeks and you’ll be back at the front. Now beat it and stop your nonsense.”

True to his word, two or three weeks later and I was back chasing the speed merchants and the great Willie Miller was nowhere to be seen. I felt great again, ready for the season ahead, and I couldn’t quite understand why I had let it affect me so badly. I recently spoke to Stuart Kennedy about it, telling him how stupid I had felt by thinking about giving up. I got the usual sympathetic reply from my mate, “If Willie had ever beaten me in training, my boots would have been in the bin straight after the session and I would never have darkened the door to Pittodrie again!” I’m assuming Stuart's application to work for the Samaritans wasn't successful!

We had it ingrained in us that losing was a terrible thing that should never be accepted, but when it did inevitably happen, you had to put it behind you and work on winning the next game. Similarly, when we won, we celebrated big style, but never believed that was the peak—we always had to keep improving. It's a great lesson that can apply to anyone in business, or even within your personal life, that when you make a mistake, you must forget that event and instead focus upon the future, or you will certainly not perform at your full potential.

I'm sure we have all seen this happen during a live professional sporting event. Goalkeepers in football are a great example where even the best can suffer, where one mistake suddenly seems to start a whole series of others, all typically causing major problems due to the nature of the position. It's the same in business, where there is no time to linger on those moments when wrong decisions or bad judgements have been made; we have just got to move on, learn lessons and not let the situation snowball. Dealing with this properly is vital, as mistakes can multiply easily; by keeping your focus on these mistakes you can drive a blame culture that will lead to mistakes not being rectified but being covered up. Then you just lose and lose again.

For us at Aberdeen, we learned how to deal with this and followed the mantra. We didn't linger on the highs or get too low during the bad times. We all knew what we needed to address and how to improve and move forward. If mistakes were made, you were told about it in the strongest terms, but you usually knew yourself, and you knew the standards that you needed to meet.

No matter how well or badly we had played, on a Monday morning we would start training and planning again for the next match. If we lost three important players to injury, the Boss would say that we would deal with it when the next game came around. He must have been thinking about it the whole weekend—who was likely to recover, who would need to be replaced and how many players would be available. This put the focus and demands firmly on Roland Arnott, the physiotherapist, to get those injured back to full strength.

In football the next measure of our success was only days away as the matches would come thick and fast, so the need was to focus on what we had rather than what we didn't have in our resources to meet and face the next challenge. It strikes me that it's the same in business; if you hit your weekly target today, you start chasing your next weekly target tomorrow, and you need to work with what is available to you to achieve that.

We were fortunate in a way that we won trophies quickly to convince us that we could win, and early victories helped to keep the momentum building. It's a bit like getting the low hanging fruit in business, where you target some easy achievements to kickstart your improvement process, showing early results and building confidence. I knew that we had to have small wins to instil the belief in what we were doing and to drive the way ahead. Sir Alex never talked much about losing that League Cup final, as it was a case of taking our medicine, learning from it, and moving forward. Sir Alex didn't mince his words—10 minutes was enough time for him to get the message across and leave us with the reminder that we had to do better.

We were ready for anything, and everyone at the club clearly understood our aims and targets. The Boss was managing in an environment where success couldn't be bought. He had been set his targets by the chairman when he arrived at the club as our new manager, and when the chairman spoke to him, he made it clear that it was vital for Aberdeen not to get into any financial problems. That's when he was told to work with what he had. He became the master at getting the best from everyone at Aberdeen Football Club, keeping them focused to achieve the aims and objectives of the club.

Throughout my journey at Aberdeen we built up this desperate will to win at everything, be it on the field of play or in activities that we enjoyed as a team. Everything was a competition: head tennis, snooker, dressing well or at least not dressing badly—anything! I remember getting slaughtered for a bad haircut and I knew that it was coming. I just had to sit and take it and remember not to use that barber again after that! My hairdresser was Ian Turnbull. He was part of my testimonial committee—a great lad. But that hair cut was all his fault—he suggested giving my hair "a little bit of body". I didn't do that again! Within the group it was friendly 'dog eat dog' stuff, but we were all still mates.

We had very high standards—they were needed to do what we wanted to achieve—and we knew that when they dropped, we had to do everything possible to get straight back to our very high level. Our goals were set by Sir Alex, and those were felt and followed throughout the club from the newest recruit to the most senior. You didn't always need to be told when you were failing to reach the levels required, but you still knew it was coming.

In the second round of the UEFA cup in 1978 we were drawn against Arjeş Piteşti of Romania. Having beaten the reigning champions, Bobby Robson's Ipswich Town, in the first round, we were full of confidence up against a team from a less well-recognised football country. We won the first leg at home comfortably 3-0 and looked well on course for the next round. Out in Bulgaria, though, for the return, we were 2-0 down at half-time, and as we were walking off the pitch for the break, wee Gordon Strachan said to me, "The Boss is going to go bananas. I've had a nightmare."

Gordon didn't need to be told that he hadn't played well in that first half, but he also knew he was in for it. He was always going to get a bollocking, but the Boss's attempt at setting the mood probably made things even worse. When we went into the dressing room the Boss started on him straight away. "Strachan, that was a disgraceful performance." At this point Sir Alex swung an arm in an attempt to knock a table full of cups of saucers into orbit, but instead he rattled a large tea urn with his arm. The urn weighed a ton and he only succeeded in nearly breaking his arm. We were all trying desperately not to catch his eye and definitely not to laugh. The Boss was grimacing with pain, but he quickly got back to Gordon before the moment was lost. "You don't belong on the football pitch, you belong in a circus. It's like Barnum and Bailey out there."

Unfortunately, Gordon had no idea who Barnum and Bailey were, but while the Boss continued his rant, Stuart Kennedy was cashing in on the fact that Gordon was the one taking the verbal battering. He stood behind Sir Alex and Archie Knox pretending to juggle balls like a circus juggler! The wee man was looking in disbelief at Stuart while being given a tough time by the Boss.

As we headed out of the dressing room back onto the park, Gordon got a hold of Stuart. "What the hell was that all about?" he asked him

"You're Barnum and Bailey, Gordon," was the reply from Stuart, but Gordon still didn't have a clue what he meant!

I tried to help. "They're a famous circus act, wee man, everybody knows them," I explained.

"Well, I've never heard of them," was Gordon's response.

He had heard the message, though. We scored twice in the second half and although we lost 3-2 on the night, we went through 5-3 on aggregate. In that second 45 minutes the wee man was outstanding. We turned the game around and Gordon raised his accountability bar. He needed to be reminded of the goals of the team and the standards required, and he turned it around in the second half. I think the humour really helped too; in any team it is important to have humour to create a feeling of being within the team, and this helps to get over the tough criticism that sometimes comes your way. It's also another reflection of the importance of psychological safety.

When I talk to business colleagues, they have all encountered similar situations in their businesses, so I remain convinced about the parallels between what happened in my footballing days with Aberdeen under Sir Alex Ferguson and today's business world.

Taking the lessons I learnt during my football career, I look at business and think the same principles can be introduced there. In business, the challenge in my opinion is not to accept second best in how you function as a business unit. There is great talk nowadays about having a clear vision, a defined mission statement and values. These are nice to have. However, for me, the key is to set clear goals and objectives as to what the business is aiming to achieve and to stand for. It is vital to set the objectives and clearly communicate those objectives throughout the organisation so that everyone at every level understands fully what is required of them and how they can contribute to the success of the business. Get everyone working together, buying in to the shared goals. Do this and then you can allow your workforce to make the right decisions because they know what YOUR decision would be.

The business acronym SMART is particularly interesting in the way that it talks about goal or objective setting. It tells us to set targets at many key levels that are Specific, Measurable, Accountable, Realistic and Timebound if you want to be successful.

A business, just like a sports team, should carry the desire to excel. What excel actually means will differ depending on the context or maybe the size of the organisation, so you will need to define that, but it will need to be what is required to keep moving the business forward to become the best it can be.

Sir Alex Ferguson showed this desire from the minute he walked through the door at Aberdeen Football Club, making it clear that winning trophies was absolutely the goal for us. One trophy would do to start with, but we would build and continue to build from there to become greats on the European stage. That desire didn't exist prior to the Boss, and possibly it could be argued that the earlier teams under different leadership were simply accepting of what they did and how they performed. We always wanted to win any game we played, but I don't think we quite imagined what level of success we could actually achieve. We didn't have that vision of greatness that could drive us on to better things. That changed completely with the arrival of the Boss. Sir Alex clearly had no intention of leading a football team without achieving success.

I have tried further to get my head around this, and when I look at those great footballing days with Sir Alex Ferguson, clearly there were some SMART objectives, not that anyone ever referred to them in such a way. And yet I, the team and the organisation knew that to be successful, there was a need to clearly understand the main objectives. Interestingly the only real goal the Boss was given by the chairman was not to get the club into any financial difficulty. Sir Alex set his own goals for the football team; he refused to accept the team being simply second best, and we all knew what we needed to do, as it was clearly communicated to us.

While we never talked about having SMART objectives in the way that a business would do today, looking back you can see clearly how it fitted everything that we were about. The great thing was that these objectives were relevant to every game we played; the objective to win was very clear, very *specific*, and was equally *measurable* through the result. *Accountability* went to each of us on the park to make it happen by doing our jobs, and indeed the entire playing staff had a responsibility for making it happen through the tactics that we discussed before the match. I've also heard of A standing for 'Achievable', and that was equally applicable, as we didn't try to become the best team in Europe overnight; it was a series of steps and wins to get there.

The objective was undoubtedly *realistic* and *timebound* as we focused on one game at a time and for the 90 minutes we were on the field, we knew that when everything came together, we could beat anyone.

In business, the challenge is to make your SMART objectives something that you work towards all the time. They're not a statement that you make or announce and then revisit a year later to see how you got on and who you can blame for failing to achieve your goals. And they're not a poster for the benefit of visitors or your senior management team. They should drive your behaviours every day, as the whole team strives to hit these targets. Failing to do that can make damage to a business inevitable.

In my opinion it is vital for a business to have a clear

vision to move forward and to know what to aim for. SMART objectives can be over a fixed period of time, providing the business with a series of specific aims and objectives. Objectives that are measurable. Individuals who are accountable in achieving the overall objective, and objectives that are equally realistic and timebound.

Our success was measured by the trophies that we won and successes that we achieved; everyone from the top at Pittodrie to the newest member of staff was accountable for their actions toward the common goal. The targets were realistic at the time, which allowed us all to buy in to them, and they were timebound. We had games to win, all adding up to the season-long goal that we set out to achieve. One of the most cliched comments in football is 'We're just focused on the next game,' but this is all about achieving your short-term goals. You can see from how managers use squad rotation that it isn't really true these days anyway. Managers know they need to have key players ready for particular games and the team that goes out onto the park must be at 100% fitness. It involves a level of planning and looking ahead that gives a lie to the 'one game at a time' idea. When the short-term goals are properly aligned to your long-term goals, they will point the way to success.

I was recently talking with one individual who had lost his business, resulting in his family losing everything that they possessed. He even lost his car and had to get a bike to get around instead. When he eventually found work it was 70 miles away. Unable to buy somewhere to live closer to his new job, he had to spend three years living with his mum and dad, leaving his wife and children on a Monday morning to go to his new place of work by bus before returning again by bus on a Friday night.

There were many other sacrifices that his family endured during those three years, and he was just one of many people who suffered because of the closure of his business, having previously employed 23 other people. The failure had an effect on more than just himself and his family they were all impacted, as were their families.

We spoke about what went wrong with his business and he told me that, looking back at it in the cold light of day, he had no clear understanding of the journey that the business needed to travel, no objectives or plans, no roadmap for success, and he simply tiptoed through playing the game of being in business and being a business person.

In fact, the only clear goal that he ever applied for success was to write the business and financial plan to raise the funding to buy the business.

This should have been his template for success and should have been the foundation for the plans and goals that needed to be made and achieved. These plans should have been reviewed on a regular basis and amended as necessary, taking into account the success or otherwise in hitting the targets and changes in the business environment. However, this was never done.

Four years after successfully raising the funding to buy the business, he had to place the business into Members' Voluntary Liquidation—it had gone bust.

When any sort of business operates, including a football club, it clearly has to keep a close eye on the financial operations. Sales, expenses and profit are areas in which to measure success, and the other is the liquidity of the business, demonstrated within the balance sheet of a business. Is there enough cash to pay monies owed, to put it simply? When there are insufficient funds, technically the business is insolvent. This was the case with Members' Voluntary Liquidation, and that impacted his business, which was unable to pay its debts to suppliers, etc.

With a clear roadmap for success and referring back to the business plan, which was his template, things may have been different. He and his family would not have struggled for many years, nor—and he has never forgotten—would the other 23 personnel who worked in the business.

In business there is a need to understand what the aims and objectives of the organisation are. What is your SMART objective? It may be for a team or an individual or a business and could involve business planning, financial planning, unit or departmental objectives for the operation or the financial forecasts that drive success, be it to increase turnover by 10% year on year or simply to survive; to finance a lifestyle or to make millions. And it is vital to communicate the journey to everyone within the organisation or business.

Of course, I have simplified this; however, be it in sport or business, clear goals and ambitions will drive the roadmap toward whatever successes you strive for. It is fundamental to have that clear roadmap that some call a vision. Have a vision, as Sir Alex clearly had, and believe in it. Continuously review it against set parameters—the measurable part.

Goal setting is therefore key and is a continuous and living process. Goal setting should be considered as a moving target and continuously appraised and measured at strategic points to measure where we are at against where we said we were going to be. This measurement process is fundamental.

These stories and my experience under Sir Alex Ferguson go a long way to highlight how important goal setting is to achieving success. While there may never be explicit mention of SMART objectives, without drive and vision Aberdeen Football Club may never have become the number one club in the world in 1984; this was according to published UEFA statistics at the time, ahead of teams such as Liverpool, Manchester United, Juventus, SV Hamburg and Barcelona. It's easy to forget that we really were that good!

CHAPTER 8
Getting Emotional

WHEN I PLAYED FOR Aberdeen Football Club there was never any talk of what is today known as Emotional Intelligence; what it was and what it stood for. Back in my days at Pittodrie, emotional intelligence had never even been heard of, let alone anyone knowing how to implement the concept into the business of running a football club. Looking back now, though, with a bit of experience of the business world and understanding some of the important methods that are out there, I can see the actions and behaviours that the Boss exhibited would have fitted the term emotional intelligence. I'm not sure that Sir Alex would have been aware either that his actions fitted into that terminology, but looking back now, all the clues were there in how he went about his job each and every day.

What I have learned about emotional intelligence is that it all boils down to being self-aware and understanding yourself, about how we feel at given moments in time and being open to understand, and appreciating those feelings. It is also about understanding the feelings and emotions of those that are around you and being able to tune in to them—that ability to be empathetic. Looking at it in a broader environment, like sport or business, it is also about understanding the team; how are the team? How are they feeling? What are their emotions? How are they impacting relationships within the team? Managing these relationships during the ups and downs of life is crucial if a team is going to be successful.

If you look at the example of family life, those of us with

children can relate to how we feel or have felt with a child that 'pushes our buttons'. We can internally feel angry, but how we then react and deal with the issue is the important part. We can also relate to our children in that we can tune in to the behavioural clues that they display at times when they want feeding, when they are tired, when they just want attention or to be entertained. This empathy allows us to understand and take the necessary supportive action by giving them food, playing with them or just listening to them. Take it a stage further and we can all, then, appreciate and manage relationships; it just needs a bit of putting yourself inside the mind of the other person or people and not just judging them by their actions. Even if you have not experienced this within a family environment, there are very similar experiences that are evident in the workplace or in any team.

Even without the concept of emotional intelligence, it was evident to me that Sir Alex could tune in to me and the other players to get the best out of us day in, day out, both individually and as a unit.

Not that he always managed to demonstrate emotional intelligence in every set of circumstances! There are many stories that everyone will have heard that show that at a given moment in time there was a break in the theory. Just like with families, there will have been times when we have been the victims of poor emotional intelligence. These things do happen; however, it does not take away the fundamental issue of being a good parent or a good manager, whether that's at a football team or as the leader within a business.

We used to play in a reserve league on Mondays and Tuesdays, and the team comprised of a mixture of first teamers who needed games to grow their match fitness, reserve players and lads from the under 18 squad. These games were an ideal opportunity to gain match fitness, but also for a player who was coming back from an injury to get some game time or for someone who had not been selected for the first team match on a Saturday to play some minutes and to hopefully impress the manager and coaching staff.

Archie Knox, who was our assistant manager, would drive the bus down with the squad along with reserve team coach, Teddy Scott, and the Boss would come down by car. The two of them hardly missed a game between them, watching this great mixture of players young and old, with a couple of 16- and 17-year-olds thrown into the mix as they began to make their way through the system.

One night we had a game away at Brechin, a match that we won without any problems, but after the game the Boss gave one of our young strikers a hard time. The Boss felt his first touch was poor and that he hadn't been making the right runs off the ball for most of the match, so he laid into him big style. When the Boss had finished giving the young lad his dressing down, Teddy Scott asked Sir Alex if it was alright if he could talk to him away from the dressing room. He said, "Boss, I'm not trying to do your job for you, but when we go back up the road, that young lad is going back to his digs in Aberdeen and a flask of tea and biscuits. He comes from Glasgow, he's only 17, he's not got his mum and dad to go home to and you've just destroyed him." I had been there myself, 17 years old and staying away from home in digs, and it's not always fun, so I could imagine how the boy was feeling at that moment.

Immediately the Boss said, "I never thought on that, Ted." He realised that he had got it completely wrong on this occasion and no doubt approached the young man to repair the possible damage that had been done. He respected Teddy a lot, as did all the players and staff, and he learned a lot from him.

Leadership is a multi-faceted talent, and emotional intelligence is a huge part of that. It allows all the other factors to come into play. While not everyone is naturally blessed with emotional intelligence, each of us has some of it within us. We just need to be aware of it and work on using it, which will improve our leadership qualities, which in turn will drive operational excellence in everything that we do. In Aberdeen's case, as a football club, the qualities of emotional intelligence shown by Sir Alex Ferguson, his understanding of the people around him and how to relate to them, led us to significant international recognition and success on the pitch over a number of years.

A huge part of how the Boss connected with everyone at the club was those daily chats with all the staff. That really must have made everyone feel a million dollars, the Boss taking the time to talk to them, listen to them, take an interest in them and have a laugh with them—it wasn't just about the business. Every time I see a business manager or leader these days, I look at them and wonder how many of the people who work for them they actually know. I mean *really* know. It's a good question that I'm sure will resonate with a lot of people who feel that they've been forgotten in their jobs, people who don't think they've been recognised for being part of the big wheel.

Fergie enjoyed these meetings too—it wasn't just a case of fulfilling some function of his job—and that would have come over to the staff. We felt this from him too, all the time, maybe in a slightly different way, though. When he joined us for a game of cards, snooker or whatever, he showed that he was part of the team. However, it was clear he wasn't just doing it for that reason; he was always desperate to win and we were always desperate to beat him! Sometimes we would have to gang up on him, especially at cards, to get him out of the road. It was hard to talk about him when he was sitting beside you!

One of the great things about Sir Alex was that, despite his huge focus on winning and making the club successful, this approach to people, his use of his emotional intelligence, wasn't something that he just switched on and off for his own benefit. He was absolutely brilliant with me when my mother died during the middle of a season. We were due to travel to Glasgow to play Celtic on the Saturday, and naturally there was no way that I was going to be in any fit state to play. The Boss knew how important my mother was to me, especially having raised me and the rest of the family mostly on her own. He also knew what I was like as a person, so he called me and suggested that I should travel with the team to Glasgow and, as the Boss said, "Just sit in the dugout and watch the game, get away from it for a few hours." It was a brilliant touch from him and really helped me at the time. It just goes to show how he related to the people around him when he could take time out of his schedule preparing for the match to think about me.

It was exactly what I needed and it certainly helped. It took my mind off things for a little bit of time and it was so important that he understood me, how I was and what I needed at that point. And by putting me first on this occasion, when I most needed it, he once again strengthened my loyalty and commitment to him and the club, even if that was never his intention.

As I look back at the influence that the Boss had upon me, I always wonder how his skill in understanding others was developed and where it came from. It was evident in other great managers of a similar era, such as Bill Shankly at Liverpool, Sir Matt Busby at Manchester United and Jock Stein at Celtic—all of whom enjoyed great successes with their clubs.

Jock Stein was one of the greatest managers in British football and was highly respected and regarded across the world. His incredible record at Celtic included ten League Championships, eight Scottish Cups and six League Cups, and was topped off when his team, made up entirely of local Scots, became the first British winners of the European Cup in 1967. Remarkably, Jock played a key supporting role for us at Aberdeen at the final of the Cup Winners' Cup in 1983, although we didn't know it was going to happen until the last minute of the game. Our opponents in that famous final in Gothenburg were Real Madrid, who, as I've mentioned, were managed by another great in Alfredo Di Stéfano. The Argentinian born Di Stéfano was such a good player that he was capped by three nations—Spain, Argentina and Colombia! He is still to this day regarded by many as one of the best footballers of all time and is best known for his achievements as a player and manager of Real Madrid, where he is still revered. He was instrumental in the club's domination of the European Cup and La Liga during the 1950s; he scored in five successive European Cup finals during that time—a record that will surely never be broken.

The aura surrounding Di Stéfano was indescribable, and seeing him on the training ground before the final would have taken our attention away from our preparation for the biggest match of our careers. It would have been the sort of occasion that the selfie was invented for! The Boss knew that this was a risk too, but as usual he had planned for it in advance.

So, we were on the training ground and who walked in but Jock Stein. Sir Alex had invited him along with two thoughts in his mind: one—it would keep our minds away from Di Stéfano while we listened to some great advice from Jock, and two—the opposite happened, as the Spaniards were distracted by the presence of Big Jock! It was another masterstroke by the Boss, and it helped us to focus on the business at hand - winning the game. The Boss knew how we were feeling as we approached the final, and this very simple act helped us in many ways to overcome any anxieties that we may have had or pressures that could have got in our way.

Sir Alex had the same understanding of the youths back in Pittodrie as he did with the first team players. Those younger boys, aged between 12 and 16, who were on S forms were needed to become the future of Aberdeen Football Club, so the Boss kept a close eye on them too. He would wind them up terribly when he got the chance, using humour to establish a relationship while often driving a message home as well.

The kids would be treated for any injuries in the same way as the senior players, using the treatment tables alongside the first team players. The Boss would frequently come in to the treatment room to see what the situation was and he would have a joke with the younger players.

"So, what's wrong with you, wee man?" the Boss would ask.

"I've damaged my hamstring, Boss," was a common reply from the kids.

He'd give them a doubting stare. "You've got a hamstring at your age?"

That broke the ice and levelled the playing field, a clear

indication of an individual who understood how to break the barriers and make people feel comfortable. He was full of empathy too. On another occasion I heard a young player telling Sir Alex about an injury that he had picked up and the Boss was full of understanding. "Yeah, I know how you feel, son. I once played with a broken back, you know!"

I'm not sure that it was actually empathy that we thought he was full of after making that comment!

The banter and human approach to dealing with people at every level in the club stemmed from Sir Alex and set a template that contributed to us feeling all part of one large team. At Gothenburg, despite us being completely focused on preparing to win the greatest prize in the club's history, on the day of the game the Boss had arranged for all the players' wives to come to the stadium to see us. What a boost that was for us all!

Working with my business colleagues, I have looked at how this modern thing called emotional intelligence is utilised within the business world. There are many, many successes that we have seen where empathy, understanding ourselves and others and how we manage ourselves in differing situations, for example, contributes to success. People are complex beings, but when you get it right with them, you are in a position to create something fantastic, just like Fergie did.

Businesses these days have mission statements, visions, culture and all sorts of other modern terms developed with the help of years of research by successful companies. None of that was really talked about at Aberdeen Football Club, but you can look back now and see that the ideas behind the terminology existed. Perhaps the fact that the board of directors at the time told Sir Alex Ferguson just to manage the team and not get the club into debt was setting the top-level mission statement, but of course Fergie had a vision that went way above that. He created his vision and let the whole club see what it was. From that moment on, it was the people throughout the club who would go on to make the difference, buying into the vision and the targets that we needed to hit in order to achieve it.

Looking back at the earlier example, where the lack of a clear plan and set of targets contributed to the failure of a business, it seems that not using emotional intelligence within the workplace contributed greatly to their problems. That is despite the fact that he is one of the nicest people I know—a naturally caring, thoughtful individual. However, he didn't realise that applying his social and personal way of life was equally appropriate in the workplace, especially in terms of how you look after people. At work he thought that his job was to make profit by generating sales, and that didn't leave time for his most important asset—his people. Although it was a private company and there were no shareholders to appease with their dividends, the principles of running a business are fundamentally the same.

The very fact that he had disregarded the people that he employed, and instead focused more on his own success and recognition in the local community, played a large part in the eventual downfall of the business operation. Goals alone are not enough; you need the method to achieve them and the staff on side to make it happen. You do that by taking the time to understand them, what makes them tick and what hurts them. You make them a major cog in the wheel, a real part of the business. Building that relationship is crucial, and something that Sir Alex did brilliantly.

In this example, and there will always be many more that others have seen, my colleague's focus was clearly not on the people. The very fact that he went through the motions of having the odd night out and occasional team building day away from the office really had no impact upon the effectiveness of the business. Whilst his staff all received their monthly pay and carried out their tasks appropriately, there was a deeper resentment toward him and to the business that, while giving them a livelihood, did not make it the best place to work.

In the space of just a year, 4 key people, out of a staff of 23, left the organisation. That heralded a decrease in sustainability and signalled the downfall of a business that had been established in the town for 11 years.

They say that you learn more from your mistakes than from your successes. Hindsight has 20/20 vision, and on reflection, the fact that the business collapsed and he learned from it provided him with the greatest gift; to understand that people are key to a business, whether it be a football team, a sports team, an organisation or a department.

At Aberdeen—and undoubtedly given his success, everywhere that he went—the Boss naturally used the key elements within emotional intelligence. He had this fantastic social awareness, the ability to understand the individual characteristics of the people that worked for him. He used that to create fantastic relationships with his people, relationships that are largely unbroken to this day. He had great self-awareness, knowing what he could do to influence those about him. For example, that look at his watch during what became known as 'Fergie time'. And, of course, he could manage his character to get the best out of people without having to resort to bawling and shouting at them. Yeah, OK, maybe the last example had its exceptions!

In Aberdeen Football Club, my professional experiences under the leadership of Sir Alex Ferguson clearly demonstrated that all of these elements usually worked in harmony. Those four same qualities also spilled over into my private life, and just like Jock Stein was the guiding light for Sir Alex, and as the Boss was to me, I am now the guiding light for my children and grandchildren.

As the late internationally recognised American author and civil rights activist Maya Angelou once said, "I've learned that people will forget what you said, people will forget what you did, but people will never forget how you made them feel."

CHAPTER 9
A Change is Gonna Come

SOMETIMES EVEN THE GREATEST of changes occurs by accident. Alexander Fleming was said to have discovered the properties of penicillin by chance, enabling one of the most important developments in the medical world. But great leaders understand the need for change, create the environment to allow changes to happen, and by letting their people see and buy into their vision, they stimulate the opportunity for improvement. Or, as in Fergie's case, they demand it.

As I've mentioned, when the Boss arrived at Pittodrie in 1978, I was the first player that he met. I worked in the stadium at that time to supplement my wages and I knew a bit about him because of the success that he had achieved with Paisley club St Mirren. He took St Mirren from the third tier of Scottish football to the top flight, winning the old First Division on the way.

After a year of working with the great former Celtic captain Billy McNeill as our manager, we were all excited to see what the new boss would bring.

Billy had set the club on a good path, finishing runners up in the league and the Scottish Cup in 1978, results that were celebrated around Aberdeen and saw some fans labelling the players as legends. It was a title that I rejected instantly because I realised that, despite the improvement in the team and the performances, ultimately there were no prizes for finishing second. When Sir Alex took over, it didn't take long to realise that he thought the very same way as me; he wasn't prepared to accept being worthy runners up. We were here to win.

Sir Alex made his vision for the club very clear straight from the start. This winning mentality that he instilled throughout the club—to be the best at everything you do - was bought in to very quickly. We all shared this vision, even if at first it seemed daunting, but he convinced us that we could get to the very top. He didn't overwhelm us with unachievable expectations, but the manageable goals that he set showed the pathway to the very top of the game. We were going to be a one-trophy team, then a two-trophy team, then a three-trophy team and so on.

The possibilities were exciting, and we all wanted to be part of it. We even created our own version of performance incentive bonuses. We would meet at the ground to travel on the bus to away games, with some early starts if heading to Glasgow or beyond. Once on the bus to away games, and usually before we had even got out of Pittodrie Street, our full back Stuart Kennedy would shout out, "Chocolate biscuits tonight, lads, not Rich Tea." This was our code for getting a win bonus, because if we won, we would be able to afford the very best biscuits that night to enjoy after our dinner—none of your cheap rubbish biscuits for us! Something that can look so minor was hugely important to us. I'm sure that anyone in any job will understand that it's these little touches that can inspire and motivate, but sometimes business leaders can miss the importance of this. Fergie didn't, and of course he made sure that the celebrations were shared throughout the entire club.

So, crucially, we had all been convinced of what we could achieve as we started on this exciting journey with the Boss. But he knew that it would take more than just addressing the winning mentality within the team. We would need to change the status quo in Scottish football. Rangers and Celtic had won every league title and most of the domestic cups for the previous decade and a half. They were the big Glasgow institutions, financially strong with huge crowds backing them, and they had a massive revenue stream. They also seemed to have, in many people's eyes anyway, an undue amount of support from the football authorities, the referees and the media.

To change our fortunes, we would have to learn to deal with that.

Having played for Rangers in the 1960s, Sir Alex was aware of the impact that a large, passionate fan base could have on a club and on football matches, and he saw this as an opportunity for change at Aberdeen. When he arrived at the club there only seemed around five supporters' clubs—this for a club that was said to have the biggest catchment area within British football at the time. The whole of the northeast of Scotland and the Highlands was prime territory for Aberdeen, as this was before Inverness and Ross County had teams in the senior league. Fergie set out to capture this market, galvanising the public to take more of an interest in their local team. He encouraged the creation of supporters' clubs all over the area and supported them by attending events and making sure that a couple of players would go along to meet the fans and continue to inspire people to come to the games to make themselves heard and to drive on the team. There would, of course, be financial benefits for the club by maximising attendances and a far greater opportunity to sell merchandise to a wider fan base. But it was more than just that; it helped to instil a passion and belief that comes from everyone being part of the club, and that passion would help in the battle to overcome the mighty Old Firm: Rangers and Celtic.

Breaking the Old Firm dominance, though, wouldn't just be done at our home games in Aberdeen when our vocal support would be the majority; we knew that we would also have to be able to go to Glasgow and win. This, according to Fergie, meant that we had to beat the opposition, their fans, the officials and the West Coast media. We were developing a team with some of the best players in the country; Miller, McLeish, Strachan, Archibald and many more—players who would play numerous times for their country on the world stage. Great players in their own right, so we should have been able to compete on a level playing field, but the field wasn't flat. We had to change an attitude that it was OK to lose in Glasgow. That happened with the constant battle to be winners, but the Boss helped us to develop a siege mentality to overcome all the other odds.

Initially, when refereeing decisions went against us, which we always felt they did against the Old Firm in particular, one of us would give the referee a mouthful and end up in the book for it. That would leave that player on a knife edge for the rest of the game, so we soon learned to gang up on the ref – if six of us were giving him abuse, he wouldn't know who to book and the pressure would be much greater on him to think again next time a contentious decision came up. Our thinking was simple—if we didn't stand up for ourselves, the referee would be influenced more by the other team and their supporters, and key decisions would go against us. This would result in us dropping points that we should have won. Many people had seen at first-hand how this had worked for years for Rangers and Celtic, so we needed to do the same.

The 1979 League Cup final against Rangers was a clear example of how good the Old Firm were at it. That game could have gone either way until the Rangers striker Derek Johnstone collapsed on the ground, claiming that he had been smacked on the back of the head by Doug Rougvie. Dougie, the Ballingary Bat as we called him, protests his innocence to this day, but the antics of the Rangers players made sure that he got his second yellow card of the game and off he went. The numerical disadvantage proved too much and we went on to lose our first cup final under Fergie. Dougie was inconsolable, but, of course, he would get his own back with numerous victories over Rangers and Celtic in the years to come.

My colleagues now talk about a business thing they know of called the rule of 23. It simply means that you have to reinforce a message something like 23 times for it to really stick, to become something people would know and do without thinking about it. The Boss might not have known about this, but it fitted his way of doing things perfectly, constantly driving the same message into us until we, or at least most of us, took it in and acted upon it. Fergie was always aware of the impact that the section of the crowd at Celtic Park known as the Jungle could have. Before our away games against Celtic, he would always tell us not to antagonise them, just to keep them quiet and hopefully stop them getting fully behind their team. Every time, it was the same message. They were a noisy bunch, a threat to us and a fantastic support to Celtic. Maybe Dougie didn't understand what antagonise, meant though, because he would run out onto the pitch and warm up in front of them; star jumps up and down the length of the terracing, facing them. They went crazy at him every time, but it was like water off a duck's back to the big man.

Situations like that defeat to Rangers, and losses of that magnitude, would provide inspiration for the future under Fergie. It was examples like that he would be thinking of when he was teaching us how to react on the pitch. He had a magnificent way of getting the importance of it over to the players. "What would you do if someone stole your wallet out of your pocket?" he asked us. "You would chase them, wouldn't you? That's what the referee is doing with these decisions. He's stealing your win bonus!" Willie Miller, of course, became famed for supposedly playing refereeing games. I guess he really appreciated his win bonuses!

He also saw the press as part of the problem that had to be solved to make us a great team. Back then, Aberdeen wasn't the easiest place to get to from Glasgow, where most of the national press were based. Again, because of the size of Rangers and Celtic, the successes they had enjoyed, and their huge fan base that was spread across the country, they were the darlings of the national media. The back pages would be filled with stories about them and their achievements, designed to appeal to the masses, and naturally helped to sell newspapers. Fergie's view was that the press hated Aberdeen and they hated the journey up to the city to report on games, especially when we became a threat to their favourite teams.

He also saw the prospect of playing in Europe, midweek games in the middle of winter on cold, cold nights in Aberdeen and that difficult journey up there and home again late at night as something that he could use. He knew that the journalists didn't want to be there sitting in the cold, reporting on a team that wasn't 'theirs', before driving back down the road and getting home at about three o'clock in the morning. So he used this as added motivation for the players. "The last thing these people want is to be coming up here to watch us," he told us, "so let's make sure they have to keep coming up here!"

We did that by being successful, by winning games and advancing in Europe. We never felt, in the early days at least, that we got the respect that we deserved, a fair crack of the whip from the press, so we were more than happy to go out and make this happen. We also knew that we had a choice. The Boss said to us after an early European exit to think about what it meant. "What would you rather be doing on a Wednesday night, watching *Coronation Street* or playing in Europe?" Not much of a choice really!

The Boss created change across the whole club, causing disruption that would shake up Scottish football and lead us to the very top of the game. Of course he had to do it on a budget, an issue that was well managed by the then chairman Dick Donald. Football progress at the bigger clubs is often based on spending money to buy the best players; initially, Fergie was keen to do this, but Mr Donald set him a clear goal with that early bit of advice that he had given him—"Whatever you do, Alex, just don't get us into debt." So the Boss had to work cleverly and find other areas that he could influence to make a difference, and he realised that there were opportunities within the youth system.

We were on the cusp of bringing some great players through the established system that we had. John Hewitt, Neale Cooper, Neil Simpson, Eric Black, etc. were still young kids but would break through during the early years of Fergie's reign and, most importantly, were given the opportunity to play in the first team by the Boss. It was rare to have so many talented youngsters within the system, and the Boss recognised this. He made sure that they mixed with the older first team players at training, developing their competitiveness along with their skill, but despite giving them the same responsibility on the pitch and at training, he was always a bit more parental towards them.

We were staying at the Inverclyde Sports Centre at Largs prior to a semi-final, not long after Fergie took over. We had all been sent to our rooms at about ten p.m. to rest up, so myself, Stuart Kennedy, Gordon Strachan and Alex McLeish settled down for a game of cards—we usually played been Hearts—before we put the lights out. Half an hour later the Boss knocked at the door and stormed in. "What do you think you're doing?" he asked us.

Stuart took control and replied, "We're just having a wee game of cards before we go to sleep. It helps us wind down. We'll be finished in 15 minutes, boss."

Fergie looked around at the four of us and stopped at McLeish, still not happy. "What age are you?"

"I'm 19, boss," came the reply.

"Right, finish off and get to bed," he said to us as he pulled the door shut behind him.

Literally two minutes later and he came through the door again and shouted, "I thought I told you lot to get to bed."

Kennedy again was the voice of reason. "Yes, boss, we're just finishing a wee game of Hearts. Nobody's drinking or partying. We'll be done in 15 minutes."

Sir Alex surveyed the room again and Big Alex caught his eye once more. "What age are you?" he asked once more.

"I'm *still* 19," came the instant reply, leaving the rest of us in stitches. The Boss slammed the door shut with one final warning to us to get to bed—even us older ones!

No matter which way you look at it, it's hard to say that his treatment of the youngsters was anything less than beneficial. One of that group, John Hewitt, would of course go down in history after coming off the bench in the Cup Winners' Cup final to score the winning goal in extra time against the mighty Real Madrid. This was after Eric Black had scored earlier, while the two Neils formed the dynamic engine room that powered the team to glory over many years. Simpson, in particular, had a great habit of popping up with vital goals just when we needed them.

Fergie could see this talent coming through, but

he wanted more. Again he realised that there was an opportunity to disrupt the norm, to break away from the established way of doing things. He would also want to take any opportunity that he could to get under the noses of the established big guns and our closest rivals. So, there were huge opportunities to achieve both things when he decided to expand the youth training camps. Opening a training centre for the kids on the doorstep of Celtic Park in Glasgow must have really caused some friction down that way, but of course it also gave us access to a huge number of young players. That would greatly increase our opportunity to find the next big stars.

A conveyor belt of young players was created across the country to support the future development of the club, supporting the occasional clever purchase of established players. Although this was no trial, I believe that it provided the template for Fergie and his class of '92 at Manchester United when he had the confidence to bring the young David Beckham, Paul Scholes, Gary Neville, Phil Neville, Nicky Butt and Ryan Giggs into his team and to win the league down there. After all, about 12 of the Aberdeen squad that won the Cup Winners' Cup final in Gothenburg had come through the youth system, while six of them were under the age of 21. He knew that it could be done, no matter what Liverpool legend Alan Hansen thought about never winning anything with kids!

Disrupting the market, the status quo, was brilliantly done by Fergie, as it should be by any business leader trying to grow their organisation. If you always do what you always did, you'll always get what you always got, as the saying goes. We had to break up the Old Firm duopoly; we had to change from worthy losers to winners. Sir Alex created that possibility by changing the way that we did things and by changing our mentality as well.

Clear goals and a shared vision of what we could achieve were a vital start. We weren't frightened by this because the expectations were manageable, growing each year as we proved what we could do. We were rewarded along the way to recognise our successes—even with chocolate biscuits! My business colleagues have used a variety of 'trophies', from cinema vouchers to stock options, and notably the simpler ones were just as effective. Cinema vouchers had the obvious advantage of lower cost so that they could be handed out more frequently, and in a way were more visible than stock options, so would be gladly welcomed by the recipients.

From his playing days with Rangers at Ibrox, the Boss was well aware of many of the aspects that made a club like Rangers so successful—attributes that also applied to Celtic and any other dominant club. He had done his analysis of what made his competitors successful and he knew that he would need to change us to be able to compete with them. Expanding the supporter base was an obvious example that will apply in any business, but he recognised this doesn't just happen, you have to make it happen. He brought people into the fold by selling what was on offer, sending players out to visit an expanded surrounding area and creating a bigger market. For businesses nowadays, there do not need to be any limits, with the internet and social media making almost anything possible. And while it's not always possible or relevant, I believe that he showed that human contact is a great way to help this along.

Of course, some things that Fergie did won't apply in the same way to businesses. Setting out to deliberately antagonise the media worked for us because it became another common goal, but it's unlikely to be advisable in most cases! However, it did change the norm again, and it got us more prominence in the newspapers and on the television, all of which helped to increase our profile and expose us to a new audience. Identifying how to get this increased exposure, getting a friendly contact or even changing your advertising focus, could benefit any business.

With us, of course, the idea was about creating unity within the club, building a siege mentality. Ultimately, it's all about getting everyone pulling together, and it's the leader's responsibility to work out what will work best to achieve that for their organisation. A small local retail outlet could rally together against the Amazons of this world; IT services would have their battles against the giants of their sector. Building belief in the team that you can take on the big guns, just like we did with Rangers and Celtic, is possible, at least at a certain level. And once you start achieving your manageable goals, you may well find that the next set of goals can take you to levels that you never believed possible.

Talent and attitude will be at the core of any organisation, and Fergie made sure that he maximised both of these attributes. Money was tight, as it always is in one way or another, so he changed the way that the club found its talent pool. By doing this he greatly expanded the areas in which he was looking and developing his players. He would also use his extensive list of contacts to find the best talent out there, and once they came to the club, irrespective of age, they were absorbed into everything that the established players were part of. The mindset and attitude spread throughout the club, with winners being established at all ages. The approach to recruitment and player development had been changed completely.

CHAPTER 10
Got To Get A Message To You

COMMUNICATION IS A VITAL leadership attribute and one that many people often fail at. It is the way that key messages are delivered to improve performance and to achieve results. How they heard and understood is key. The delivery of the message has to be such that it reaches its target and enables the correct actions to be taken.

Anyone who has ever observed the Boss from afar could quite correctly predict that his messages never suffered from misinterpretation! "Send reinforcements, we are going to advance," would never morph into "Send three and sixpence, we are going to a dance!"

However, this only touches on how the Boss articulated his messages and instructions. Whilst he could be short and direct, that was only a small part of his communication skillset.

The Boss's feedback at half-time and full-time was always short, to the point and about affecting what was to happen next. He did not dwell on the past, which was obviously only minutes ago, but rather who needed to do what and how, to make things better in the second half. Other managers may prefer to wait until things are calm before discussing in detail what happened. In fact, it is not uncommon for managers to wait until players return to training on a Monday and then have a calm sit down with various analysts to go through what happened 48 hours ago. Maybe it was just that group of Aberdeen players, but we reacted well to the immediate feedback. Yes, it could get lively, but everybody was there, and recollection of events was not corrupted by time passing.

In my opinion, more importantly, there was no danger of individuals creating diversions or excuses. With enough time, people can usually find a way to reasonably justify things that have gone wrong! Even if there is a good explanation, often the message still needs to be heard and not mitigated. You need to find a way to succeed no matter what barriers are in front of you. From our point of view it was good that the feedback was soon over, so we could begin looking forward to the next game or the second half with a really effective message ringing in our ears.

There was the odd occasion where the Boss was so concerned by our performance that we would get dragged in the day after a match to get the benefit of his wisdom. We went in one Sunday after a 1-1 draw with Hibs and everyone got it that day. The smart money is usually on keeping your head down, taking your medicine and moving on, but someone like Stuart Kennedy tended to bite back. When Fergie got round to him, he obviously wasn't happy. "As for you, you were pathetic yesterday, Kennedy!"

Stuart considered this very briefly before responding, "Pathetic, am I? He then looked over to Steve Archibald and asked him, "Hey, Stevie, see that cross I landed on your head? Was that pathetic?"

Archibald didn't get the chance to answer, or didn't take the risk of answering, before the Boss followed up. "Don't try to get out of it. Archie, tell him he was terrible." Archie Knox just kept his head down as usual, trying not to get caught laughing by the Boss.

Stuart, of course, wasn't finished. "I thought I was pathetic? Now I'm just terrible? That's good, I've improved considerably in less than a minute! " Stuart continued giving other examples of his final pass.

Fergie had heard enough. "See you, Kennedy, you'll be playing for the reserves on Wednesday night!"

Stuart took it in his own inimitable style. "Aye, but I bet you'll have me back in the first team when we play Celtic on Saturday!"

True to form, he was back in his usual place against

Celtic, even after he told the fans on the Wednesday night why he was out with the reserves. "I'm only here because I'm a nightmare, by the way!"

Obviously, the situations at half-time or full-time were not really appropriate for extended two-way debate! However, away from these high-energy moments, the Boss was always willing to hear what you had to say. Whether it was related directly to a match performance or a personal issue, once you met with the Boss you always received his full attention. A very good example of this was not long after he had arrived from St Mirren, where he had been manager for four years. Initially the Boss had, in the players' opinions, a really annoying habit of comparing our match and training performances unfavourably against what he thought he had at St Mirren. He would try to coach us by saying, "This is what Tony Fitzpatrick would do" or "Frank McGarvey wouldn't have missed that".

These guys were good players, but what really annoyed us was that St Mirren couldn't get near us and we didn't feel that there was very much that we could learn from them. Stuart Kennedy, as always, had his say: "St Mirren hardly win a corner against us."

Our recent record against St Mirren had been fantastic, so we were just fed up with the comparisons. Following a brief discussion amongst the more senior players, it was agreed that our team captain, Willie Miller, and Stuart Kennedy himself should approach the Boss on the topic. Of course, we were all a little nervous as to how this approach would go down with Sir Alex. We wished Willie and Stuart good luck and sent them off to see the Boss. He agreed to meet them and listened to what they had to say. Willie and Stuart pointed out how the Boss kept making these comparisons with players at a team who we were dominating at the time, and if he kept it up, the players were likely to switch off and stop listening. He listened attentively to what was said, remained calm throughout the meeting, and when the boys had finished, he said that he didn't realise he was doing this or the negative effect that it was having on the team. He promised to stop doing it, and true to his word, from that day we were never compared to St Mirren or any other club's players. Active listening in action!

There are many examples of this, some of which are referred to in other chapters. He really did appreciate honest feedback himself and would act accordingly—a trait that will surprise many people.

Of course, there are other ways to communicate, not just verbal. I've read that 55% of the the impact in communication is non-verbal, and even as a young manager at Aberdeen, Fergie had immense presence. The ability to walk into a room and immediately command 100% attention is an amazing trait to have and is very powerful. During my time as a professional footballer I had two managers who evoked such a response, one obviously being Sir Alex, and the other was Billy McNeill.

Billy McNeill was and is the most iconic player ever to play for Glasgow Celtic, having been the captain of the famous Lisbon Lions, the first British team to win the European Cup. So, what gives a manager this presence? In my opinion it is not their physical demeanour. Although this may impact your first impressions, it will not last unless, and this is what I think is crucial, they can produce results consistently. Many football managers over the decades have created their own images; the flamboyant one, the grumpy one, the funny one, the special one! However, unless they produce results consistently, their image will evaporate.

The Boss had a great little habit that he developed to keep us on our toes and prepare us for his arrival. I've been in dressing rooms where the manager would walk in and the players would just keep their conversations going until he managed to get their attention. That wouldn't happen with Sir Alex, though. Just before he got to the dressing room, he would produce a loud cough before entering. Whether this was conscious or not, it sent a signal and prepared his audience for his arrival. When he walked in, we were ready for him and he was ready for us; his tone and facial expressions always matched the circumstances.

As said so often throughout this book, Sir Alex is first

and foremost a winner. He looks at every aspect that can influence a game, and primarily that was his own players. But, of course, he left no stone unturned, trying to eke out any advantage or opportunity that he could get. While he might have been screaming at us players to get up and down the park, keep tight to opponents and push to the end, he had some famous non-verbal communication methods as well. Most famous of all was the telling look at his watch right in front of the fourth official who was responsible for setting extra time. The look didn't suggest more or less time to be added, but rather shorter or longer depending on what suited his team. The old saying that a picture paints a thousand words—or in Sir Alex's case, a look says a thousand words—is very true. If you want to work out how effective this non-verbal communication was, you only have to google 'Fergie Time'—it's in the Urban Dictionary now!

As mentioned earlier, Sir Alex tended to make his feedback short and to the point, and his preparation for games was very similar. For most matches we would receive some simple instructions and information regarding our opponents, and maybe even referees, but essentially, he simply trusted everyone to do their job, to do what we were good at. When required, however, he would provide a short, detailed dossier on our direct opponents. This was typically when playing in Europe, where our knowledge of our opponents was limited. Archie Knox did a great job pulling these together, making sure that they included the important information that we needed. The dossier would have descriptions of our opponents' strengths and weaknesses, where they tended to position themselves on the pitch and a couple of diagrams to highlight these. Typically, this could run to about four or five pages, all good stuff that the players had to take away and absorb prior to the game.

All in all, the Boss was excellent at communicating; it was simple, it was accurate and he would listen if challenged. All of this was underpinned by the trust and loyalty that he built.

Of course, he communicated and influenced anyone who could play a part in the club's success. When he was the manager at St Mirren, he would go around the town encouraging the good people of Paisley to go to the next home game. And, of course, at Aberdeen he encouraged the players to attend supporters' club functions, dramatically increasing fan registration and therefore home attendances, pushing the team on to greater performances. Everything was always geared towards winning.

The Boss quite clearly had mastered the art of communication. Typically, people describe this as the combination of verbal and non-verbal, but I would take his ability further. He could communicate without speaking or even being present. The consistency and expectations that he had were such that you pretty much knew what was going to be said before you met him. Just like I knew that I was likely to be under scrutiny following the pram incident and big McLeish dropping me in it. Gordon Strachan obviously did as well during that game in Romania that I mentioned earlier. At least the wee man got the opportunity to make amends out there, as the Boss kept him on for the second half. He duly rewarded Fergie's decision by scoring as we came back to draw the game 2-2. Sometimes when you look back at it, you think the Boss was strong in all forms of communication; verbal, non-verbal and he was probably even telepathic! He certainly knew how to get into my head!

CHAPTER 11
You Got The Power

EMPOWERMENT IS ANOTHER TERM that is used a lot in business these days. It's another phrase that is often used without the meaning being properly implemented. In team sports like football, though, played in a real time, dynamic environment, we all had to be empowered. Even if we didn't know what it meant!

Empowerment can be defined as 'authority or power given to someone to do something'. A lot of what goes on in business relies very much on the idea of creating an environment where people are empowered to make decisions. We want individuals to make decisions, confident in the knowledge that it is the right thing to do for the organisation and knowing that they have the power, ability, and responsibility to make decisions.

This takes us right back to psychological safety again and is a huge reason why we need this. Making decisions involves risks. It is unlikely that we'll always make the right ones. They have to be made in the context of what is happening at the time. People may be under pressure, and with various options to choose from it can be difficult to choose the right one. Yet people still have to feel they can make the decisions that lie within their empowered zone. When people have been trained, given a structure or a system to work with, they just need that safe environment to know that they will make the best decisions they can.

I'll give an example. In two minutes my whole life changed, as did those of my fellow players and colleagues at Aberdeen Football Club. It was a change that was felt throughout the entire city and the wider community too.

In fact, if I put this into business speak, every stakeholder connected to Aberdeen Football Club also benefited from those two minutes.

So, what happened?

On 2 March 1983 we travelled to West Germany to take on Bayern Munich in the first leg of a quarter-final tie in the European Cup Winners' Cup. Bayern Munich were a powerful and dominant force in European football at that time, just as they are now. With a squad packed full of international players, we knew that this would be a really tough game—about as hard as it gets. A couple of years earlier, maybe we would have felt a little intimidated, as we'd had some bad experiences against West German teams who maybe weren't as good as Bayern.

But we were a team that had grown and had learnt lessons from all the defeats that we had suffered. Fergie picked a team to do a job that night and made a decision to leave Gordon Strachan on the bench. Despite chances for both sides, the game finished 0-0, with the West Germans looking amazed by the tactical awareness that they saw from a Scottish side. It was perfectly balanced for the much awaited second leg that was played at Pittodrie a fortnight later.

The West Germans were quite rightly considered a mighty force to reckon with and still would have been favourites to win the tie and progress. It looked very much like they believed that too, as they seemed to have a swagger and a strong belief in themselves. At the time, Bayern had won three European Cups and one Cup Winners' Cup, whereas we had yet to win a European trophy; it would have been easy for them to look at Aberdeen as a small Scottish club with no great history in the European arena. During the build-up to the match, while we were training and planning, we heard stories that the West German players were wandering about Union Street in the city centre buying lovely crystal gifts as mementos of the trip. Was this a sign of overconfidence? Maybe even arrogance?

The game would go down in history as the greatest ever match at Pittodrie. The plan was to keep it tight, but that only lasted 10 minutes, unfortunately, as Augenthaler scored a screamer from outside the box to leave us trailing. We were level half an hour later, though, as Eric Black's elastic neck managed to keep a cross from Mark McGhee in play, and it fell to Neil Simpson to bundle home the equaliser. One all and all to play for.

We went in to the second half knowing that we needed to win the game on the night now, as away goals would favour Bayern. Our task became even harder 16 minutes into the second half as Pflügler restored Bayern's lead with a fantastic volley from the corner of the box. With half an hour to go, we needed to score twice.

Big problems require big decisions. The Boss identified that the issue we were having was that we were not getting enough good quality balls into our opponent's penalty area. He was getting worried and wanted me on the pitch. He reckoned we weren't getting the ball forward quickly enough and he had a plan to make that happen, so he decided to change the team around.

I was standing waiting to go on and the substitute board went up with number two on it, signalling that Stuart Kennedy was to be the man to make way. Stuart saw the board, and being unaware of the Boss's plan, wasn't happy at the idea of being substituted. He shouted to Sir Alex, "I'm surprised that Bayern are taking their right back off. I thought he was doing OK."

Fergie shouted back at him and told him it was him that was being substituted. "I'm no coming off. Take someone else off," came the reply from Kennedy!

"Just get aff, now," insisted the Boss! After what felt like an eternity, I finally got onto the park.

Stuart will still argue to this day that it was a mistake!

The Boss wanted me in midfield to put long balls into the opposition penalty area, putting the West Germans under greater pressure, so Doug Rougvie moved to right back to cover for Stuart and Neil Cooper went to left back.

Ten minutes later, John Hewitt came off the bench to replace Neil Simpson. The Boss had made his decisions and rang the changes, which left the 11 of us on the pitch with the responsibility of going out to get the win. In the 77th minute of the game we were awarded a free kick on the right-hand side of the field. What happened next became an iconic piece of play in the history of the football club. It became the most famous free kick in the history of Aberdeen Football Club. Gordon Strachan and myself stood over the ball about 20 yards from goal at the Paddock End of the ground. We knew that we had the ability; we knew that we had been empowered and we took the responsibility.

Gordon was right footed and I was left footed, so with both of us standing over the ball, the Bayern defence were left wondering if it would be an in-swinging or out-swinging free kick. They marked our players tightly to cover all options.

Or at least they thought that they were covering all options. As we were discussing who was going to take the free kick, Gordon said to me, "We're going to muck it up." That was the clue.

There had been a couple of good free kicks earlier in the match that had come straight off the training ground, but this was something else. Gordon and I both ran to take the kick at the same time and both of us ran over it. We stopped and looked at each other in amazement as if something had gone badly wrong. At this point the pushing and bumping of players on the edge of the box stopped momentarily as the players there began to reset. The West Germans were probably laughing at us inside their heads, thinking we had just messed up a great attacking opportunity. Suddenly, while the defenders were distracted and their usual disciplined defensive set-up was disorientated, Gordon wheeled around and whipped a perfect cross into the box. Alex McLeish had given himself a couple of yards of space while confusion had reigned in the defence, and having made the run past his opposition marker, he got his head on the ball to score the equalising goal. Game on—2-2.

To this day I am often asked if this was a planned routine. Yes, it absolutely was. It had been created by the Boss and Archie Knox and we trusted their foresight and creative ideas. As a team we had planned this and practised it over and over again, knowing that at some point a situation would occur where we could make it work. The Boss then knew that he could trust us to use our decision making on the pitch to deliver when the time was right. When Gordon and I discussed it, we sent a signal to our teammates about what was going to happen, while the Bayern players just thought we'd made a mess of it.

With only 13 minutes of regular time left on the clock, we were drawing with the mighty West Germans, but that, of course, wasn't good enough. The two 'away' goals that Bayern had scored meant that, as things stood, they would qualify for the semi-final and we would be out. We needed another goal to progress. The West Germans had been left stunned by our mad equaliser and we knew what to do on the field of play; the tactics had been changed by the Boss and we were left to make the decisions that could impact the game.

The celebrations on and off the park were wild and the West German players were stunned. Johnny Hewitt, of course, just about the youngest player on the pitch, wasn't getting caught up in celebrations just because the scores were now all square. He knew that we still needed another goal and time was running out. He wanted the ball back on the centre spot, so rushed into the goal to retrieve the ball and threw it back to the middle of the park.

As Bayern kicked off the match, we swarmed them, trying to take advantage of their shock at being conned by our free kick routine.

Adrenalin rushing through us all now, we needed to get on the ball again as soon as possible, so we mugged them straight from the kick-off and regained possession. The ball quickly made its way to me on the halfway line down the left-hand side of the park. Now it was my turn to decide how to use the instructions that the Boss had given us. We hadn't been getting enough good quality balls into the box. But that was about to change. I hit a 50-yard diagonal ball behind the defence, where it was met by the head of Eric Black and his amazing stretchable neck. The crowd rose to their feet and screamed in delight, only to see the ball come back off the bar. Just as joy was about to turn to frustration, Johnny Hewitt appeared on the scene to knock the ball into the back of the net. This time he wasn't following the ball in to get it back—we were now in front. Hewitt wheeled away, revelling in the celebrations like the rest of us this time.

Just two minutes after trailing the West Germans, we were now ahead for the first time in the tie, and we knew that we wouldn't be caught.

The joy was overwhelming. As it stood, with just 12 minutes left on the clock, we were heading for the semi-final of the European Cup Winners' Cup and leaving the great Bayern Munich in our wake. By now we were in complete command, and the final whistle soon sounded to confirm our progress.

Job done!

One of the greatest nights for the football club. We had beaten one of Europe's greatest sides and we were off to the semi-final. The post-match celebrations were joyous but limited to a couple of beers in Bridge of Don for me. There was work to do starting the very next day. Enjoyable work, to be fair, and even the Boss was in great spirits. We were still challenging for the league title and had progressed in the Scottish Cup too, but by now we knew what the next stage of our European adventure would be: Waterschei of Belgium in the semi-finals.

Was this empowerment? I think it was. The Boss had communicated to us what the tactics needed to be to win the game, and because of our individual skills and abilities, we were permitted to take the correct course of action to ensure that the objective was met. There was no need for the manager to run onto the pitch to tell us what to do when the free kick was awarded, because he trusted us to make the decision that we felt was the right thing to do at the time. Much of this is obvious, and of course it's necessary by the very structure of how a game of football works, but it does show the need to believe in your people and let them do their job. He trusted us and we trusted each other.

John Hewitt didn't wait on an instruction to get the ball

back when it went into the net. If he had not done this at that moment, the outcome could have been completely different. And then, of course, I had to pick my moment to play that long ball into the box. In those two minutes it all came together perfectly; an amazing achievement brought about by a manager who had coached his team and then watched them implement the plans when they knew that they would work.

It's an incredible feeling to look back at those two minutes and what they meant for us all. I just wish that I could watch my pass again for that third goal, but unfortunately the television cameras were still focused on McLeish after he had scored his goal. They only just caught up with play as Eric got his head on the ball!

The West Germans were absolutely deflated after the game, and perhaps buying crystal souvenirs was not such a good idea after all! Maybe a crystal ball would have been more beneficial!

There really was no difference in how we approached each game, both before and after that match against Bayern. However, those two minutes to many people will define the Business of Winning for Aberdeen Football Club and demonstrated many qualities of leadership that are equally applicable in business.

When I discuss this game, and the events within it, with my business colleagues, we have looked at what is important to allow empowerment to happen. In my opinion, one of the key elements when you allow individuals to make decisions is that they feel they are in a psychologically safe environment. While decisions can be reviewed and potentially criticised, they shouldn't be ridiculed. If the decisions aren't correct, then obviously there needs to be feedback—more training may be needed or better procedures required to improve this in the future. Every decision needs to be taken in context, but if a business is clear about its goals and objectives then it can allow those members within it to make decisions. Of course, managers and leaders can guide and seek understanding as to why the decisions were made, but if we talk of empowerment, it is about giving the individuals permission to do what they believe is the right thing to do without fear.

I heard a great example from a friend of mine about how he was empowered and took the initiative that came with it. He was a student who had a part-time job working in a hotel. While he was at work one day chatting to the chef, there was a delivery of fruit and vegetables that arrived from a local supplier. The supplier was a bit stressed out and explained to the chef how he also supplied to the Royal Household at Balmoral Castle when the Queen was in residence. He was bemoaning that there had recently been a problem delivering to them, and he wasn't sure how long he would be able to continue.

By coincidence, my pal's family also ran a fruit and veg business in the area and he thought he saw an opportunity. Although he wasn't involved in the business at the time, he called his father, who ran the business, and explained what he had heard and wondered if there might be an opportunity for them. His father, who liked what he was hearing, saw this as an opportunity not just to get a prestigious order but also to get his son more involved in the family business. He told him to look into it and follow up on it if he thought it had legs.

Just like the 'mucked up' free kick when we saw the opportunity and grabbed it with both hands, so did my friend in this situation. He had been given the opportunity and had been empowered to take it forward. He sensed the need to seize the chance and felt that he was responsible for making it happen, with the possibility of providing a very tangible competitive advantage to the family business.

That led to a series of events that drove him to write to the Royal Household at Buckingham Palace, offering to supply Balmoral Castle. They heard nothing for three years until one day he received a call from his father saying that the Royal Household had been in contact directly with the business and they had placed an order.

That initial order was delivered and after a few years of further supply, the business was recognised as a Royal Warrant holder as suppliers of fresh fruit and vegetables to

Her Majesty the Queen. That's a nice medal to have in your business trophy cabinet!

This example is perhaps different, but it does highlight the benefit of allowing individuals within a business to have a degree of free flow and empowerment to take actions as they see fit for the benefit of the business. Of course, situations need to be managed, and not every decision made will be the correct one. However, the very fact that you make somebody feel empowered to strive forward with ideas and decisions is a vital way of making that business more effective and operationally successful.

That is what the Boss did for me and my fellow teammates. He and Archie Knox provided the path to success and gave us a clear sense of purpose with clear objectives. He himself was given lots of leeway to make decisions in the running of the club, with that simple instruction from the board of directors to not get the club into debt ringing in his ears to provide some limits.

It allowed him the freedom to make the decisions, and he himself was empowered. That drive and purpose filtered to all the staff at Pittodrie, who then felt empowered to make the right decisions on and off the pitch.

Empowerment breeds importance, and importance breeds commitment and excellence. I love the story regarding President John F. Kennedy and the janitor, one that has since been used as an advert on television. JFK was visiting the NASA headquarters for the first time in 1961. While touring the facility, he introduced himself to a janitor who was mopping the floor and asked him what he did at NASA.

"I'm helping put a man on the moon," was the janitor's brilliant response. He showed great awareness of the bigger picture. He could clearly see how his work contributed to the organisation's goals and objectives.

But these principles go back even further. You might have heard the story of Christopher Wren, a seventeenth-century English architect, who one day walked unrecognised among the men who were at work building St Paul's cathedral in London, which he had designed.

"What are you doing?" he inquired of one of the workmen.

The man replied, "I am cutting a piece of stone."

As Wren went on, he put the same question to another man, who replied, "I am earning five shillings two pence a day."

To a third man he addressed the same inquiry. "I am helping Sir Christopher Wren build a beautiful cathedral," was his response.

That man had vision. He could see beyond the cutting of the stone, beyond the earning of his daily wage. He saw the creation of a work of art—the building of a great cathedral.

If we provide individuals with a vision, clearly communicate this vision and help them to understand it, we can then rely on the rich talents within any organisation or sports team to make the right decisions.

This is empowerment. This is what was so evident on the night of 16 March 1983. Gordon and I knew that our job in the 77th minute was not merely to take a free kick. Our job was to win the football game. And that we did!

CHAPTER 12
You Have To Admit It's Getting Better

GIVEN THE AMOUNT OF scientific, engineering and academic expertise that has driven business for hundreds of years, it can be difficult to imagine that sportsmen, often with little or no education beyond the age of 15 or 16, could influence business. Even beyond some of the Fergie examples that I saw, though, football has often been ahead of the curve.

Continuous improvement is a great example. Something that only started gaining business traction, in the West at least, in the mid 1980s had for years been standard practice in football. The best teams never stood still; it was very rare for even the league champions to start the following season with the same squad that finished as winners just a couple of months earlier. Players were added and players were moved out, with a clear understanding that staying the same would mean going backwards. That dominant Liverpool team of the late 1970s and early 1980s is a classic example. Club greats like Jimmy Case and Terry McDermott were moved out even though they were still very capable of doing a job, and they were replaced by younger talents who were expected to keep Liverpool on top.

We have probably all seen the examples of what happens to businesses when they don't continually try to improve, when they get set in their ways and think that times aren't changing. They struggle to understand that 'good enough' isn't actually good enough. This can be seen from High

Street brands to high technology; Greggs replaces your local bakers and Amazon replaces the bookshop next door. Even when you do create something that is massively successful, you have to immediately look to make it better, more efficient, and offer more to the buyer. Look at the iPhone—what version are we on now? And what version are they currently working on? It's a process that never stops.

The same is true in football and always has been. When the Boss arrived at Aberdeen, of course he didn't have that high bar starting point, as he wasn't taking over the champions, but he did have a good squad. He made it very clear where he wanted to get to. And he made a very clear indication of his desire for continuous improvement with the goals that he set. "We'll be a one-trophy team, then a two-trophy team, then a three-trophy team," he told us.

That good squad included some legends, like Joe Harper and Bobby Clark, but not all of them had a long-term future at the club. Fortunately, Fergie wasn't one to throw the baby out with the bath water. He gave some the opportunity to get on board with his programme while building the infrastructure behind the scenes. He had a succession plan to bring through new players who could replace the stars of yesterday—players who would fit into his vision of a winning team. There would be no mass clear out, just a measured amount of change, a little bit at a time.

Wee Joe was one of those players who would need to be replaced. Joe scored well over 200 goals during his senior football career and was loved by the fans, but age was against him when Fergie arrived at Pittodrie. The Boss was also worried that Joe had too much influence on some of the players around him and was maybe too set in his ways and unable to change. Cliques in a football dressing room, no doubt the same as in any environment, can cause issues for the entire team with the potential to disrupt the progress that the manager was making. This came to light after a 2-2 draw against Hibs when we played badly. After the game, lots of players were sounding off about what had gone wrong, and the Boss told us to report to the ground the next day to sort it out.

When we arrived the following morning, the Boss gathered us all on the pitch and told us that this was our chance to say what we thought had gone wrong. There would be no recriminations, everyone was free to have their say. Wee Joe started the feedback by criticising the formation that we had played, saying that we should have had Stevie Archibald up front alongside him instead of playing further back in a deeper role. He was quickly supported by Stevie, Dom Sullivan and Ian Fleming, three of Joe's closest associates who all lived in the same Westhill area of Aberdeen. The Boss managed to hold his tongue for about five minutes before he'd had enough and ended the get-together. After the meeting, he turned to his assistant, Archie Knox, and said, "See those bloomin' Westhill willy biters . . ."

Within 18 months all four had left the club, despite the no recrimination promise! However, the problem was that Fergie had seen an issue, not with their criticism, but with a little close-knit group who had the capability to upset the togetherness and dynamics of the team.

His mind was probably made up that day, but still he took 18 months to make the changes, as he knew that he needed those four until their replacements were ready. During that time, Joe still made his mark in the league winning side of 1979/80, but by that time Mark McGhee and Stevie Archibald were well established up front and John Hewitt was nearly ready. Eric Black was the next to come along and helped improve the team following the departure of Archibald. Steve had arrived at Aberdeen from Clyde for a fee of £30,000 and moved to Tottenham Hotspur for £800,000. This tidy profit was used by the club to build the South Stand, although we always referred to it as the Steve Archibald Stand!

The transitions became seamless, supported by the burgeoning youth system that kept a conveyor belt of talent coming through, all driven by the Fergie mentality of the Business of Winning. While always trying to improve the team, though, Fergie was grateful for the contributions of those he let go and would do what he could to ensure that they could still have successful careers in their own right. He was brilliant at recommending players to other clubs, and many went on to not just earn a living from the game but to win trophies as well. Ian Angus was a great example; a useful midfielder who was in and out of the team for a number of years at Aberdeen, he went on to star for Motherwell when they won the Scottish Cup in a classic 4-3 victory over Dundee United in 1994.

Goalkeeper Bryan Gunn was another. Always talented enough but stuck behind Jim Leighton in the queue, Bryan moved to Norwich City, where he starred for 12 years. He captained the Canaries, finished fifth in the old First Division and reached two FA Cup semi-finals, as well as gaining half a dozen caps for Scotland.

Andy Watson played almost a hundred games in five years at the club before transferring to Leeds United. He returned to Scotland to play for Hearts, where he was 10 minutes away from winning the league title until Albert Kidd scored twice for Dundee in the final match of the season.

Joe Harper, though, was a fantastic model of continuous improvement within a sporting environment and a great example to anybody earning their living in any business. He scored so many goals at the top level of the game, was capped and scored for Scotland and became known as the King of Pittodrie. Everyone would say that he was one of the best natural finishers in the game, but what many don't realise is that this predatory striker routinely stayed behind after training to work on sticking the ball in the back of the net. Natural ability only takes you so far, and Joe knew this.

Joe was also great with me, encouraging me to join in with the post-training sessions. He would tell me where to deliver the passes and land the crosses. I recognised my weaknesses too. I was never blessed with pace, even before that knee injury against Liverpool, but I could look at people around me and learn from them. I had people around like Jim Hermiston in the early days and Stuart Kennedy latterly, and they were great people to learn from. Jim would have me doing half-hour sprint shuttle runs with him after training, while Stuart's fitness levels provided me with the inspiration to run all day if necessary.

And did it work?

Well, I went from not getting a game for the reserves to starring on loan at Peterhead, then into the first team at Pittodrie, winning the Premier League, the Scottish Cup and then the European Cup Winners' Cup. It seemed that the more I practised the luckier I got, as someone famously once said! But again, all this was based on the huge culture of winning and being driven to improve all the time to achieve that. I'd like to think that I personally had the mental approach already within me to strive for continuous improvement, but that isn't the case with everyone.

That's where leaders come into their own, but not just with your typical after-dinner motivational leadership speech. We've probably all heard something, usually from an ex-sportsman like me, telling a few funny stories and saying, "You're great, go for it!" These stories are often fantastic, entertaining and provide an insight into a top achiever's career, but that sort of motivation typically struggles to have an impact that lasts much longer than the duration of the dinner. Motivation to keep improving requires setting the right kind of environment, with regular and routine reinforcement needed, knowing that will make it happen.

Fergie was fantastic at reinforcing a message.

It's easy to believe that when you progress to a good level of your chosen career, whatever that may be, you don't need to keep learning, but you can always take something from people around you. The great players that I played with were always looking to develop further, and we would share lessons even during games. Again, the great Joe Harper was a fantastic example of this, a clever footballer whom I enjoyed playing with. During a game against Rangers, with the score still 0-0, he came up to me on the pitch and asked me to try something. He had noticed that the great Rangers defender Tam Forsyth was following him all over the park, so he told me that when he dropped short there would be a huge gap behind. Rather than playing the ball in short to his feet, he wanted me to play it into the gap and then leave it to him.

Five minutes later I received the ball and saw Joe make his move with Tam indecently close to his backside. I knocked the ball over the top and Joe spun, leaving Tam in his wake. He was on it in a flash and clear of his marker. A second later he played it across to the inrushing Steve Archibald. With an air of inevitability, the ball was in the back of the net to make it 1-0 to us. Continuous improvement, even in the madness of a huge match.

Coming from the shipyard town of Greenock and returning there in 1986 to play for the local club, Morton, I was able to witness at first hand the collapse of the shipbuilding industry. Shipbuilding was to Greenock what fishing was to the northeast of Scotland around Aberdeen; at its peak there must have been around 20,000 people working in the yards. I would have been one of them had it not been for football. I was doing my apprenticeship there when I was spotted by the Aberdeen scout in the area, John McNab. John watched me for 18 months at Parklea playing fields in Port Glasgow, where I was playing for the local juvenile team, Port Glasgow Rovers. Parklea was virtually on the beach in the wettest town in the world, but John was there regularly with his brolly up, watching and monitoring my progress

He was great for me, not just getting me signed but he would even take me to the local restaurant, L'Arlecchino, and advise me on what I needed to do. Thanks to John I got my chance to move and play football for a living. If that hadn't happened, I could have been like the vast majority of those 20,000 workers who found their world collapsing in the 1980s. Shipbuilding had moved on, with competition throughout the world, and the local yards had failed to develop and keep competitive over time. The yards closed down and local unemployment rocketed. They had been amongst the best in the world, but failure to build on success and striving to improve all the time brought that success to a painful end.

Fortunately by then there was a new industry in town. The electronics boom was in full flow, and Greenock had IBM and National Semiconductor, plus a large supply chain to support them. The electronics industry was cash rich at this time and these large American corporations were the dominant forces in the market, but just like the shipyards, there was increased competition coming from all over the world.

By the end of the 1990s, my colleagues, who worked for National Semiconductor, were facing at first hand the reality of dealing with a situation where good enough wasn't really good enough. They were part of an organisation that was good but not good enough, and closure was on the cards for the Greenock factory. They had improved, but not by as much as the competition. Factories in eastern Europe and the Far East, Taiwan in particular, had redefined world class. A local management team was left in charge of the factory while plans were made to close it or sell it off, but this new management had other ideas. Being almost entirely local themselves, they naturally shared a common goal with their employees to preserve the factory in some shape or form, keeping local people in work and providing hope for future generations. They started a process of continuous improvement with a greater sense of urgency, utilising the talent within the factory and learning from talented people elsewhere too.

There was a huge focus on improving productivity, and targets were set and met. Their equivalent of 'one trophy, then two trophies, etc.' was to 'reduce costs to x, then reduce costs to y' and so on, with a clear focus on what the result needed to be to become amongst the best in the world. They learned that the business equivalent of a scouting system was vital—being able to identify the levels the competition were at, how they were able to improve and to use that to take the required steps to beat them.

Communication throughout the workplace got better, and workers buying into the plans had a massive impact in driving the success. This was a huge lesson in itself when they realised just how many good ideas could come from within the workplace. It's similar to the story that England's Rugby World Cup winning coach, Sir Clive Woodward, talks about in the evolution of the skintight rugby jersey.

Jason Robinson, a winger, went to see Woodward after a match against Scotland. Recently converted from Rugby League, Robinson noticed a difference in the Union code where, rather than tackle him, the opposition just needed to grab his jersey and hang on to it to slow him down. He was one of the fastest players in the game and reckoned that if the opposition hadn't been able to pull his shirt, then he would have scored a hat-trick of tries. Sir Clive listened and discussed it and then took the idea of skintight jerseys to the manufacturer, Nike. Two years later, wearing their skin-tight shirts, England were top of the world and nobody was holding on to Jason Robinson anymore.

Great ideas often come from the people doing the actual job. They experience the issues first hand and know what could make it better. Great leaders give their people the space, opportunity and confidence to promote their ideas. They also need to create that culture where people want to contribute, which goes back to so much of what I've written already—a safe environment where ideas will be encouraged and welcomed. A shared vision of where the organisation is going that has been bought into by everybody. Achievable targets that everyone is striving to attain and recognition of success.

Many jobs were unfortunately lost at National Semiconductor in Greenock, but a lot were saved, and the improvement plans were successful. Within five years the factory was rated in the top 5% in the world, the improvements continued, and despite the company being sold a couple of times, it continues to flourish today. It serves as their winners' medals, giving the new generations hope of work for the foreseeable future.

Sometimes it needs that shock or threat to your success, your place at the top of the tree, to spark the understanding that you need to change. In sport, league tables, points gained and lost, and winners' medals are easy and obvious measures to track your progress and watch the competition. Businesses need to have their own measures and ways of tracking their performance, but the principal is the same. The Boss drove improvements wherever he worked, but then you see the recent change in Manchester United and their fall from grace since he retired. However, it now looks like they may have had their shock and realise that they need to restart an improvement process to get back to the top.

CHAPTER 13
From Gibshill To Gothenburg

LIFE IS FULL OF twists and turns, a series of *Sliding Doors* moments where every choice that you make can affect your future. As a young kid growing up in the Gibby, did I ever have a plan of where I wanted to end up? And not that it was the end, but could that young kid possibly have dreamt about a journey from Gibshill to Gothenburg?

The now defunct European Cup Winners' Cup was the reward for the national cup winners across the continent. With only one team from each country, the champions, qualifying for the European Cup at that time, the Cup Winners' Cup was comprised of many quality sides. It was often the case that the teams who competed in it were on the rise and by the time the competition came around they would be amongst the best in Europe.

We qualified for the 1982/83 competition, thanks to our 4-1 victory in the Scottish Cup Final over Rangers at Hampden. We had been on a great run at the time, winning our last eight league games, but lost out on the league title to Celtic by just two points. Ironically for me, two defeats against Morton, my hometown club, had cost us the championship. Three extra time goals sealed the Cup win, though, and after a short summer we could start to dream a little bit about the glory of playing in Europe. We had been through our learning curve in Europe, had taken a few beatings, but every one of them taught us lessons—the Boss made sure of that. The previous season we beat Ipswich Town, the UEFA Cup holders, so we could see we had made progress.

Still, our status in Europe wasn't that high, and we were

one of four teams with an early start in the competition. Along with the Swiss club Sion, who we were drawn against, Swansea and Braga, of Welsh and Portuguese cup holders, we played the preliminary round in August 1982.

Sion had won their cup earlier that year, defeating Basel in the final. Switzerland wasn't as strong a football nation back then as it is now, so we were full of confidence going into the opening leg at Pittodrie. That confidence was merited, as we led comfortably by four goals to nil at half-time. We added another three goals in the second half to virtually ensure our qualification for the first-round draw, despite still having to go to Switzerland for the second leg. That second leg turned out to be a stroll in the park, or a stroll in the mountains rather, as we all appreciated the fantastic views that the Swiss landscape offered.

A month later, though, we weren't looking forward to such a scenic trip. We were drawn against Dinamo Tirana from Albania, with the first leg at home again. Albania had a fearsome reputation at the time, ruled by a hard-line communist dictatorship, and it was very difficult to get to. They made it very tough for everyone to get into the country and impossible for fans and even most of the media. Conditions were expected to be uncomfortable at best, so we had to take advantage of the home leg so that we could go there in a strong position. Dinamo were a tough team, and we only had a solitary goal from Johnny Hewitt to protect as we headed to Albania for the return leg.

Arriving in Tirana two weeks later confirmed many of our worst visions of the country. Albania was part of Europe, but this was like travelling to a third world country at the time. The locals were washing themselves and their clothes in the river, there were virtually no cars and we were worried about the food. Naturally, though, the Boss had prepared for this and had taken our own meals with us. The atmosphere, even round the hotel, was fierce, though, with the locals gathering to try to intimidate us and put us off our pre-match planning. This barely stopped. There were huge, noisy crowds outside even at midnight, trying to maximise their team's home advantage.

Stuart Kennedy must have been reading too many newspapers at the time, though, and he was worried about potential conspiracies out there. While we were warming up on the pitch before the game, he went to find out who the referee was. When he came back, we gathered around as he told us that the ref was Bela Szabo from Hungary. Of course, at that time Hungary was also a communist nation, so Stuart warned us to be careful. "Watch the tackles, lads. This guy has probably got relatives in Albania!"

Well warned, we got on with our warm-up, but Neil Simpson was curious about what Stuart had found out. "Stuarty, fars Hungary?" That's 'where's Hungary?' for the non-Aberdonian readers.

Stuart looked over as he contemplated the question, as did big Alex McLeish and Mark McGhee, waiting to see how much Stuart really knew. "Right, Neil," Stuart began. "See, after you leave Aberdeen, OK, you get to Stonehaven, then you turn left and keep going."

"Thanks, Stuarty," came the unquestioning response from Simmie! Neil must have been some swimmer!

This was all going on as we prepared for a really tough game. We remained fully focused on the task ahead, but we were also relaxed, confident in our own ability. It was a difficult game, one of the toughest that we faced in the competition that year, but we controlled it and shut them out for a 0-0 draw, which was enough to progress to the second round.

Two ties and four games down and we were off to another communist country for the next round. We were drawn against Lech Poznań from Poland, so once again we prepared carefully. We felt that our European experience was growing, having learnt from defeats in previous years, but despite that experience we still had a lot of youth in our side. The first leg was at Pittodrie again and we had Simmie, Tattie (Neale Cooper), Eric Black and John Hewitt, who all played massive parts in the game—all of them were under 21 at the time. Dougie Bell ran riot that day, and goals from Mark McGhee and Peter Weir gave us a 2-0 advantage after the first 90 minutes.

We knew that the return leg would be tough again, so we played a bit more conservatively in Poland. McGhee was left on his own up front as we packed the midfield. This allowed our wingers to drop back and support the defence. We soaked up the pressure and grabbed a goal with a header from Dougie and it was off to the quarter-finals! The big beatings that we had taken in previous years were well and truly behind us, and they were now proving to be invaluable lessons.

By now anticipation was growing about what we could achieve. We were in the last eight of a massive competition known throughout the world of football, and we felt fearless. Then the news of the draw came through—Bayern Munich. Just a decade earlier Bayern were starting out on the road to becoming champions of Europe for three years on the trot—they also won the West German championship six times in 14 years. They were true giants of world football with players known to everyone, even pre-Sky! Augenthaler, Pflügler, Breitner and Rummenigge, all names that rolled off the tongue—with a bit of practice! We were heading for the Olympic Stadium in Munich for the first leg, excited by the challenge, but we never doubted that we could do it.

I missed that first game, but it was a joy to watch. It's often forgotten because of the drama that took place in the return match, but we hammered them, even though the score finished 0-0 that night. Dougie Bell had another brilliant game, scaring the life out of them. His mazy runs were almost impossible to stop, as we well knew from training with him every day. When he did it on the training pitch, we used to sing the *Benny Hill* theme song, as that's what his running reminded us of. This, of course, was a guy we had signed on a free transfer because Fergie's replacement at St Mirren thought his skills didn't suit the brand of football which they intended to play. Their loss was our gain.

So it was back to Aberdeen with all to play for. Keep it tight, and the goals would come. I started on the bench that night, champing at the bit to get on and influence the game and not knowing how the night would turn out. The

A big hand for the 1984 double winners, including Tommy McIntyre, Ian Porteous, Stevie Cowan and Stewart McKimmie.

Neil Simpson, Willie Falconer and myself looking for whoever dumped Johnny Hewitt on the ground!

More than 17,000 fans came to Pittodrie to watch my testimonial match against a Billy McNeill select that included Kenny Dalglish, Alan Hansen, Stevie Nicol and Charlie Nicholas.

Having a breather at the end of training.

One of the last photos of me in an Aberdeen shirt before I moved to Morton.

Relaxing before the 1986 Scottish Cup final against Hearts. Looks like Wee Gordon had to start his own catering company to get into the stadium that day! He certainly wasn't getting any complimentary tickets after his move to Manchester United.

A huge Dons support enjoying that winning feeling at Hampden Park in 1986. This was the last winner's medal I collected.

After 14 years with Aberdeen I joined my home-town club Morton as player/coach.

I loved the coaching side at Morton.

After hanging up my boots in 1988, I learnt to enjoy the games from the dugout.

A montage of some of the strips I've collected, including the
Scottish League Select top— a bit of compensation for not getting a full cap.

Two legends of the game—and me! Sir Alex and Jock Stein are two of the greatest managers of all time.

It's always good to catch up with Mr Morton—Allan McGraw.

It was a huge honour to be inducted into the Aberdeen Hall of Fame!

Reunited with an old friend the Scottish Cup at an event organised by book sponsor Duncan Moir. With co-authors Robin McAuslan and Neil Martin.

With my co-authors: Neil Martin, David Christie and Robin McAuslan.

A reunion with the boys for the unveiling of the Boss's statue at Pittodrie in February 2022.

I have so much respect for the Boss and what he achieved.

atmosphere that night was the best I've ever experienced, building towards the incredible finish to the game that I described in a previous chapter.

Waterschei may not have been one of Europe's leading lights, but they had beaten Paris St Germain in the quarter-finals to earn the right to face us. Any team who reached the semi-final of a European competition would deserve respect, and that result against PSG was a useful warning to us. We were determined to get a good result at home to take across to Belgium for the return leg.

The team, especially Dougie Bell, was on fire at Pittodrie in the home tie. We dominated from the kick-off and were a goal up through Eric Black within a minute. Confidence was flowing through the staff on the bench. When that goal went in, Archie Knox sat back with an imaginary cigar and announced, "That's us in the airport, lads," thinking about the potential flight to Sweden, where the final was going to be held.

Just three minutes later and Simmie doubled our lead, with Archie again telling us to buckle up, as we were practically on the plane, ready to take off.

Two more goals in two minutes early in the second half and we were flying; wave after wave of attack was tearing the Belgians apart; even their consolation goal was undone when Mark McGhee got his second to round off the victory.

Carrying a 5-1 lead into the second leg, our place in the final was never in doubt. It seemed like nothing could go wrong, but despite an easy passage into the final, there was a cruel blow for Stuart Kennedy. Stuart had picked up a bit of a knock in the Scottish Cup semi-final game against Celtic the week before, but worse was to follow. He caught his studs in the Waterschei turf and turned his knee in what was to prove to be a career-ending injury. Not that he was having that; Stuart was never a quitter and the biggest match of our lives was just around the corner.

The Boss knew that Stuart wasn't fit; the physio had assessed him and knew how bad the injury looked. Stuart was desperate to convince him, though, that he would be ready for the final. Talk was fine, but Fergie got fed up with him going on and on and told Stuart to get outside and show him what he could do. Stuart virtually had to wait until the Boss wasn't looking to painfully get up from his seat and walk out onto the pitch, dragging his leg. Gritting his teeth, he managed a painful couple of runs before the Boss shouted at him, "Stop it, that's enough. You're on the bench!" It was a remarkable act from the Boss towards one of his key players, and it had a big impact on the rest of us. We all got a positive lift from it, as Stuart was so important to us all. It was great to see him being rewarded by the Boss, despite the circumstances. And for me, as disappointed as I was for my good mate, I realised that it greatly increased my chances of playing in the final, a final in which we would be playing the greatest club side of all time—Real Madrid.

Wednesday, 11 May 1983 is a date that will live forever in the memories of tens of thousands of people connected in any way with Aberdeen—the football club and the city. That was the day when a series of events, some planned, some fortunate, seemed to come together. Fate, in a way, but mostly it was the result of years of dedication and hard work, delivering a memory that will last forever.

We felt good about ourselves in the lead up to the game and rightly so. Beating Bayern was all the justification that we needed to believe that we deserved to be regarded at the top end of European football. We flew out to Sweden at the beginning of the week in good spirits, and we received the first sign as we checked into our hotel in Gothenburg—it was called Hotel Fars Hatt. I'm sure it means something completely different in Swedish, but this, of course, was an Aberdonian phrase meaning 'where's that?' It felt like we were at home!

With a couple of days to go until the game, we got into a routine of training and relaxing, maintaining that balance of keeping the mood cheerful and not getting bored. There was still a huge competitive spirit within the camp, even at the after-dinner quiz night. Willie Miller thought that he was a winner when asked which team has the longest name in British football. "Hamilton Academicals," the skipper shouted, only to be denied the two points because it was

'Academical' singular and not plural! Willie protested like a referee had given a decision against him, but, unlike on the pitch, nobody was backing him up this time – no points!

The day before the match, we were allowed to train on the pitch at the Ullevi Stadium, using one half of it while the Real Madrid players would be on the other half. Real had an incredible football pedigree. They would go on to be named FIFA's club of the twentieth century a few years later, six times European champions at the time when they played us, with dozens of Spanish La Liga titles to their name as well. Their team sheet was filled with world famous names, international stars like Stielike, Camacho, Juanito and Santillana. All this and managed by one of the greatest players of all time, the fantastic Argentinean Spaniard Alfredo Di Stéfano. It still feels a bit intimidating typing this four decades later, so you can imagine the potential it had to frighten even the best players back then.

But we had the Boss and the Boss had a plan. He wanted to turn the tables, get our minds off the opposition and get the Real players thinking about what was happening on our side of the pitch during training. Enter Jock Stein.

When we walked out onto the park for the training session, Big Jock walked out with us. The Spaniards were already on the pitch and you could see them turning to look at this giant of a man, known throughout the footballing world for being the first manager to win the European Cup with a British team. He'd also led his Celtic team to nine successive league titles. Meanwhile, we had spent an evening with him, chatting and taking tips and gaining confidence from the great man. We weren't interested in what was happening on the other side of the pitch now; it was all about us. We were ready for the game the following night. Big Jock was brilliant and a huge part of those couple of days. He even gave the Boss the tip about buying a bottle of whisky for his opposite number, another move designed to distract the focus of the opposition from the game itself.

We got a further boost on the morning of the game when our wives arrived. It was great to know that we had that support there, willing us on. The fans had been arriving by plane, by car and even on a chartered ferry, the St Clare. God knows what it must have been like on that ship. I heard stories of them running out of beer before they'd even left Aberdeen! For us, though, it was time to get totally immersed in the game. We had some final preparations at the hotel and then off we went to the Ullevi Stadium.

When we arrived, the heavens opened. It was pouring down. It felt like Scotland. It felt like Greenock. It felt like a game at a neutral venue that had been moved back home, presenting us with a fantastic opportunity to carve our place in history. And all this before we even saw the fans, who took it up to another level. We knew that we were going to win that game. The Boss absolutely knew that we were going to win it. By now everything was in our favour—the weather, the fans, Jock Stein, the confidence and the ability.

With Stuart unable to start the game, sitting on the bench as Fergie had promised, I was handed the number 3 shirt. Before starting the long walk from the dressing room, we listened to the Boss's last words of encouragement. "See when you come back in here after the game, make sure you can look yourself in the mirror. No pressure to do anything other than go do your job, do what you do. Do it honestly and to the best of your ability."

Walking out into that wall of noise was an incredible feeling, maybe the best feeling in the world, although only for the next 120 minutes, when it was topped. We were totally focused, but I looked around to soak up the atmosphere and to feel the expectancy of our fans. In amongst them was a large banner that read 'John McMaster Has Defence Splitting Balls!' That was a great little touch that helped with any nerves. Meanwhile, big Alex McLeish was looking at the rain landing on the park and getting a bit concerned about how it would impact the conditions. We all got a big reminder from him, "Watch the puddles, lads, no dodgy pass backs."

There were no worries about that at the start of the game as we flew out the traps. Eric Black hit the bar after just five minutes before we won a corner that was taken by Gordon Strachan. McLeish won the header in the box and Blackie was there again, fastest to react to knock the ball into the net. Only six minutes gone and we were in the driving seat. At that point we knew we still had a job to do, but the match was in our hands. Unfortunately, one player failed to heed Alex's warning about pass backs—Alex himself. Less than ten minutes after our goal, the big man played the ball back towards Jim Leighton in goal, but it got caught up in the sodden turf. The Real Madrid striker Santillana was onto it like a flash, and when he knocked the ball past Leighton, the keeper brought him down. Penalty to Real, converted comfortably by Juanito while we were still reminding an increasingly annoyed McLeish about what he had said before the game about pass backs. There may even have been a few swear words in there!

We regained our composure quickly, though, and got ourselves through to half-time with the score still level at 1-1. We walked back into the dressing room fairly happy with what we had done in the first half, knowing that we were still very capable of winning the game. You were never quite sure what the Boss would pick up on, though, or what he'd want to talk about when you got back in the dressing room, although maybe big Alex should have known what to expect.

"Pass backs, pass backs? What were YOU saying about pass backs?" yelled the Boss.

By this time McLeish had had enough of it; his veins were sticking out the side of his neck and his teeth were gritted with the pain of it all. "I know, I know! Would you all shut up about pass backs," he said.

With the message delivered and received, we could start to focus on the second half. Keep the shape, move in unison, defend with the wide men deep to close the space.

We went back out and dominated the second half, although we didn't score. I was loving it, possibly having my best ever game in a Dons shirt, in the biggest match of any of our lives. We had a few good chances that we failed to take, though, and the game went into extra time. By this time the Boss had put John Hewitt on as a late substitute, replacing our goal scorer Eric Black.

With about ten minutes left of extra time, Fergie was starting to regret his decision, convinced that Hewitt wasn't doing what he had been asked to do. Uli Stielike was trying to run the show for the Spanish team, and Fergie wanted Johnny to sit on him and stop him playing. Hewitt, though, was a forward-thinking player and his attacking instincts were frustrating the Boss. The story from the bench went that Fergie was threatening to take him off but couldn't get his attention quickly enough. Then I won a challenge deep in our half and Peter Weir picked up the ball, dancing between three opposition players to make space for himself. From there he played a chipped pass down the wing to Mark McGhee, who ran at pace to get clear of the Real defenders. McGhee's cross into the box was perfect, beyond the defender but also tempting the keeper. The goalie didn't get there, but Johnny Hewitt, still on the park, did. In normal circumstances it would have been the easiest ever chance to score, and, despite the pressure, the time of the game on the biggest night ever, Johnny finished it beautifully. The fans erupted, the players erupted, Fergie tried to join in but fell flat on his face into a puddle as he jumped out of the dugout! The rest of the bench ran over the top of him as they jumped about celebrating, leaving him there to pick himself up and dry himself off, but even he didn't care by that time.

Nine minutes to go.

Nine minutes to make history.

Those nine minutes were long but mostly comfortable until just about the last kick of the ball. Real won a free kick at the edge of the box and I lined up in the wall to face it. I'm not religious, but I tell you I was praying at that point, *please don't score. Please don't score*. Peter Weir was saying the same thing. The shot went past the wall, and we turned in slow motion to see where it was going—wide of the post!

The final whistle soon sounded and we went wild on the park while our jubilant fans went wild off it. Aberdeen Football Club had just won the European Cup Winners' Cup, beating the greatest club side in the history of European football.

We jumped for joy. We hugged and kissed each other, we ran to celebrate with the fans—this was their day as much as it was ours. I picked up a red and white tammy that was thrown onto the pitch in celebration, and I've still got it today. The Boss managed to run onto the pitch to celebrate with us, taking the time to go around every one of us to pass on his congratulations. His personal achievements were growing at a rate of knots, and he was showing just how great a manager and leader he was.

Then we reached the fabulous moment when it was time to pick up our medals and lift the trophy aloft. I think it was while waiting in line that I started to really understand just what we had done. At that point my mind drifted a bit, thinking about how I would have made my dad proud, about my mum and the rest of my family and how happy it would make them. It was great to know that Katy was there to witness it, to see what she had supported me to achieve. Then there was the pleasure of seeing the happiness of the fans who were there, and I even remember thinking what a shame it was for the fans who couldn't make it that night. At least they had the television coverage to make up for it. Picking up the trophy and parading it was amazing. When I noticed the TV camera trained on me as we posed for a group photo, I was able to send a 'hello mum' back from Gothenburg to Gibshill.

Eventually we got back into our dressing room, but I wanted one of the opposition shirts as a keepsake. I wandered back through to the Madrid changing room and stuck my head round the door, where the atmosphere was the complete opposite of ours, as you would expect. They were great champions and this hurt.

"Any chance of getting one of your tops, lads?" I shouted. The big West German, Uli Stielike, looked up, and translated my Scottish into Spanish, asking the striker Santillana if I could have his top. The Spanish international, with over 50 caps and seven La Liga titles to his name, happily obliged. Well, maybe happily is stretching it, but certainly sportingly! I didn't have the time or the presence of mind at that point to think what must have been going through their minds in there, but it showed just what they were made of that they could help me out even at their lowest point.

Back at the hotel later, the celebrations were fantastic. The Boss, Archie, even Jock Stein were all part of it as we partied into the night. The next day was even better though. We flew back in to Dyce airport and an open top bus was waiting to bring us home. As we drove back to Aberdeen, there were people everywhere wanting to see us and the trophy. When we got to Union Street, it was an unbelievable sight, the likes of which I've never seen before. The fans were everywhere, filling the streets, hanging out of windows and up on the rooftops as well. The city had gone crazy, and we were loving it just as much as the fans.

During that crazy journey that I had been on, from the highs to the lows, to the highs and back to the lows again, this was the pinnacle. Less than three years after that devastating injury against Liverpool that should have ended my football career, I was standing on top of the world. The world may have looked like a double decker bus, but trust me, it was the world that day!

This was the complete proof of what we were, what we did and how we did it. It was, for me anyway, complete proof that Sir Alex's methods worked. Every part of what he did contributed to this success, or to look at it another way, he did what he did and this was the result. No surveys or questionnaires—the proof was in the trophy cabinet. Show me your medals, indeed!

CHAPTER 14
The Super Cup

WINNING THE CUP WINNERS' CUP in Gothenburg not only sealed our place at the top table of European football while making us legends in the eyes of the Aberdeen fans, it qualified us for the Super Cup final.

The European Super Cup was a two-legged match between the winners of the two premier European trophies, the European Cup and the Cup Winners' Cup. For us, it was the next challenge on the road to being considered the best football team in the world.

For two and a half years it had been a personal challenge for me to get back playing, to get into the first team and to start winning trophies again. It needed a whole lot of hard work and determination, and the love and support of my family as well as from the Boss and Aberdeen Football Club.

The horrific injury in the European Cup game against Liverpool after the tackle on me by Ray Kennedy had a massive impact on my career development. That incident kept me out of the team for some time and, as I was to find out later on in my life, also stopped me from being awarded a Scotland cap.

It turned out that Jock Stein, Scotland's manager, had decided to include me in his next squad before the injury happened. It is a huge disappointment that I didn't get the opportunity to represent my country.

So, could we do it? Were we, Aberdeen Football Club, the best in Europe? Maybe even the world? Would all the hard work undertaken through the Boss's leadership take us to another level of excellence?

Only time would tell, and we would know by the end of the year.

The Super Cup competition was the idea of Anton Witkamp, who was a reporter for *De Telegraaf*, a Dutch newspaper. He wanted to create something new to decide definitively who the top club side in Europe really was. As he explained, it was not about the money and glory, rather it was the right to be called the best.

Although their status as a great club has fallen since, Hamburg dominated the West German domestic league in the late 1970s and early 1980s—they were West German champions in 1979, 1982 and 1983. They also won the European Cup in 1983, the culmination of several years of being a top European team. Under the excellent guidance of manager Ernst Happel, Hamburg, as we knew them, were built on excellence, experience, guile and determination. They had a formidable pedigree.

Their captain was the great Felix Magath, a ruthless player with 43 caps to his name for the West German national team, and they were managed by Ernst Happel, considered by many as one of the greatest managers of all time. Happel was one of a select few managers who have won the European Cup (now called the Champions League) with two different clubs.

At that time, many people in the UK disregarded the Super Cup, treating it as simply something that resembled today's Community Shield, a trophy of little importance. Having only been created in 1973, it was still a very young competition. However, when you look at the winners of it leading up to our victory in 1983, the names already on the Super Cup included greats such as Ajax, Dynamo Kiev, Anderlecht, Liverpool, Nottingham Forest, Aston Villa and Valencia. And although this final was simply a two club shoot out, it was a long road to get there. We had played six Scottish Cup matches to qualify for the European Cup Winners' Cup, with a further 11 games played to win that trophy by eventually beating Real Madrid. Now we had these two matches, home and away ties, against the European Champions to complete the journey.

Of course, no matter what anyone else thought, it would have been totally out of character for the Boss to consider this Super Cup as just another trophy. Rather, he had the strength and desire to be the consummate winner and to complete the next step. I think it's also fair to say that for all of us in the squad, we would have killed each other to get our hands on another trophy. A winning mentality was forever etched in our minds, in our behaviours and actions.

Being the first Scottish club to win the Super Cup was a huge incentive for us, and we were desperate to take the scalp of another great side in a European competition. While Real Madrid had represented one of the great teams of all time, Hamburg were threatening to become one of the greats of the present. We wanted that scalp.

In the first leg in Hamburg we drew 0-0 in front of 15,000 spectators in the Volksparkstadion. The Boss had us set up to stop Hamburg from scoring, using a similar set-up to the one we used in the away game at Bayern Munich a few months earlier, and once again the boys carried out the plan brilliantly. That set us up nicely for the return at Pittodrie, where 25,000 fans turned out to watch us. Roared on by this crowd, and with a more creative approach to the game, we won 2-0 with goals from Neil Simpson and Mark McGhee, both scored in the second half.

Dougie Bell was brilliant that night. He ran the West Germans into the ground with some fantastic play. For Peter Weir it was a double celebration, as his wife, Mary, gave birth to their second son that day; it was also a huge night for Stewart McKimmie, who had signed just a few days earlier from Dundee to replace Stuart Kennedy. McKimmie slotted into the team for just his second game for the club and came away with a European winner's medal.

Big Doug Rougvie took the risk of asking the Boss if the team could go out and celebrate. He must have caught him in a good mood, as he said it would be OK. The celebrations were, I can tell you, the stuff that will never be forgotten.

It's quite incredible to look back at that team now. All the players were Scottish, many of them products of the youth system, topped up with some great signings. People talk about the Class of '92 at Manchester United, who drove that club to huge success, as if the Boss had been fortunate to stumble across a bunch of kids in the system to create greatness. In reality, he was repeating methods tried and tested at his previous clubs and virtually perfected at Aberdeen. I think it is safe to say that the Boss's leadership development was completed at Aberdeen Football Club and built the foundations of his later triumphs at Old Trafford.

The Super Cup success completed a fantastic year for the club. It wasn't a bad record, was it? Taking the players to two European trophies inside five months, winning the Scottish Cup and being voted in a major football magazine in France as being the best team in Europe!

All of this was a continuation of the constant pursuit of improvement, of increasing the trophy count. That was the year I won four medals, counting that French award! It was a delight to be part of that magical era in Aberdeen Football Club's history.

The Boss was there for eight years, and during that time we won 11 trophies, turning all of us into winners and legends to this day. What an era of football for the club, especially when we beat Hamburg and were crowned champions of Europe and possibly the best team in the world at that given time.

CHAPTER 15
Coming Home

AFTER 14 YEARS AT Aberdeen, living, working and raising a family, I, Katy and our sons had become Aberdonians. The boys were settled at school and we were happy in Bridge of Don. A nice house in a nice area, doing a job that I loved.

However, moving into that fourteenth year with the Dons, I knew that it was time to start planning for the next stage of my career. Football isn't always kind to ageing players, especially given that you've still got more than half of your working life ahead of you.

The Fergie influence at this point again was huge. All the support that he had given me throughout our time together, especially when I had been out injured, gave me options. He got me involved in coaching, scouting and youth development and encouraged me to do my coaching badges with the Scottish Football Association, all long before I had reached the end of my playing career.

As I started to think about what that next step might be, I realised that I might have to step down a level or two from what I had been used to. I was really pleased to hear that both Brechin City and Forfar Athletic were interested in offering me a place at their club. Both teams were within commuting distance of Aberdeen, and, despite not being in any way big clubs, they both had a decent record of success in the 1980s. However, while I was considering these offers, I was delighted to get an offer from a footballing hero of mine, Allan McGraw.

Allan was a legendary striker for my hometown club, Greenock Morton, in the 1960s. A Govan man, like Fergie, he had been the club's top goal scorer for five seasons in a row, setting a Scottish record for goals scored in a single season in the process. He had taken over as manager of Morton a couple of years earlier. The club that had been one of our trickiest opponents had gone through a turbulent time, with a couple of relegations and a quick turnover of managers. Allan was brought in to provide stability, and he wanted me as a player-coach to support him.

I spoke to the Boss, Sir Alex, and asked for his advice. He strongly suggested that I should take up Morton's offer of player-coach, as they were in the running for promotion back to the Scottish Premier League. It would give me a great chance to put into practice the coaching badges that I had recently achieved at the SFA's world-renowned Inverclyde Coaching Academy in Largs. The academy hosted applicants from all over the world at that time, including players such as Graeme Souness of Liverpool and my old mate Gordon Strachan of Aberdeen and Manchester United fame. Even the great—or should that be special?—Jose Mourinho went there.

Taking the Boss's advice, I accepted the offer from Morton and took up a position in charge of the youths and reserves, from under 12s all the way through to first team players recovering from injuries and suffering with a loss of form. I was given free rein to work with the players, but I also had great support from the assistant manager, Jackie McNamara, the former Hibernian and Celtic player. Jackie was part time which meant that on occasions I would stand in for him in some first team training.

I loved the coaching side at Morton. Allan McGraw was a different character to Sir Alex. He was laid back and nothing seemed to bother him until it bothered him. When required, he shared the same ruthless and winning mentality that the Boss had. He let you get on with things—but you had better be successful! And one major thing came through from Allan that was so like Fergie—he cared about all of the people around him. Just as it worked for Sir Alex, Allan got more out of his staff than otherwise might have been the case.

I took the same training methods with me that we had

used at Aberdeen. Everyone got treated the same, but I adapted the pace or the length of the sessions to allow for the different age groups. There was plenty of ball work, and at the end of each session we would do 60-metre back-to-back sprints. It was kept simple, consistent and of high quality.

Of course, over time I developed some further methods, some that I invented myself and some from developments from around the world. I'm still claiming that I invented the game Tips, which was great fun but also great for your first touch in tight situations.

As I've mentioned previously, at Aberdeen, Fergie was given one clear goal by the chairman when he arrived at the club—don't get us into debt. It was similar at Morton, but for us it was a simple instruction from the chairman to sell, on average, one player a year. This would keep Morton out of debt, and as a smaller club than Aberdeen, we were less reliant on Premier League football and big crowds. To achieve this goal at a club without a lot of money to speculate in the transfer market was a challenge. We had to take our young players and develop them, which clearly was my primary responsibility.

I had 10 years at Morton, and over that time we managed to meet that challenge. Looking back now, it was quite a performance, with some great players brought through and sold on. We developed and sold the likes of Alan Mahood to Nottingham Forest, where another legend, Brian Clough, was the manager; Derek Lilley to George Graham's Leeds United; Derek McInnes to Rangers; and David Hopkin to Chelsea. You can also add Brian Reid, who went to Rangers and Alex Mathie, who joined Newcastle. We also had Mr McGraw's son, Mark, who was getting a bit of attention and inadvertently caused me to get an earful from Fergie.

Mark was a decent player and we thought we could get a reasonable fee for him, probably from a Scottish Premier League club—we were in the second tier at the time so that would have been a great move for him. One night in 1990 I received a phone call from Sir Alex, who was in Manchester. Before I could speak, I was getting a verbal battering. "How come you've not let me know about this guy Mark McGraw?"

he said to me down the phone. I could hardly utter anything in my defence when he followed that up. "Kenny Dalglish has been up watching him and I know nothing about him."

The Boss, as always, had his ear to the ground and had connections everywhere who would let him know what was going on, just like he always knew what we were up to back in our Aberdeen days. King Kenny was the Liverpool manager at the time and that made it worse—Fergie was concerned about anything that would give them the edge. This was right at the start of Manchester United's journey when they would stake their claim to be the greatest team in England, so it was serious stuff.

When I finally got a chance to speak in my own defence, I was able to explain to him that Mark was a good player who would likely go on to be successful in the top league in Scotland, but he wasn't what United needed to become the best club in England. At that point Fergie calmed down quickly, and I think he suggested I should do everything I could to sell him to Liverpool! We went on to sell him to Scottish Premier League side Hibernian, where he spent five years before moving to Falkirk and then back to Morton.

In a way it was no surprise that Liverpool had been watching Mark, as his dad was as crafty as they come. Sometimes the coaching and development of the players still needed a little bit of astute business technique to get the deal over the line, and nobody was smarter than the Morton manager.

We had another young player, Archie Gourlay, who had only played a couple of games for the club, but we thought he had a future. We lined him up for the first team in a pre-season friendly against Newcastle United, knowing that they were interested in signing him. Prior to that, though, Mr McGraw had made contact with my old boss at Aberdeen, Billy McNeill, who was then the manager of Celtic. Allan invited Billy to the game and asked for a little favour.

When the game finished, the English team's boss, Willie McFaul, joined Allan in the boardroom. He made it clear that he was very interested in our player and was ready to negotiate hard on the price to get the best deal for his club. At this point, and right on cue, there was a knock on the door and Billy McNeill stuck his head in the office and said, "Apologies for interrupting, Allan, but I need to go. Really liked that boy we were talking about, so I'll call you tomorrow to talk about it."

As Billy shut the door behind him, Allan rubbed his hands together, seeing a plan come together perfectly. Mr McFaul agreed to Allan's fee for the boy and shook hands with no further negotiation—he couldn't risk losing him to Celtic! Some say you make your own luck, and Allan McGraw was certainly an expert in helping it along! It helped our pay packets too, as we had a genuine performance bonus that was tied to hitting our targets for selling players.

At this point things were going well. People were interested in how we were doing it and how we operated on team and player development training. Obviously, my name was being spoken about in coaching circles as people saw the success that we were having. I took a call from another great in the game at the time, Jim McLean. Jim was highly regarded and often spoken about in the same breath as Sir Alex. The two of them were very similar in many ways, and despite battling it out for the major honours in Scotland, they had a very good relationship. When United came to Pittodrie, Fergie would finish his team talk and then meet Jim for a game of snooker before the game started! Not quite an Arsené Wenger type relationship, then!

McLean had made Dundee United regular challengers at the top end of the Premier League and took the club to the UEFA Cup final, having knocked out Barcelona on the way on a memorable night for the Dundee United fans. He was known for his dour exterior and had given an impression of never giving too much away. His players were tied to long contracts and probably not on the best money, given what they achieved. Jim said that he had heard great things about what I was doing, and he was looking to bring me to Dundee United to join the coaching team there. This sounded really exciting to me, an undoubted step up to a team capable of challenging for the top honours, a team capable of winning the big prizes. Obviously, this was in my DNA. He then asked me how much I was earning at Morton, but when I told him, Jim's response was very typical of him. "I'm not going to pay you that much so just stay where you are, son. You must be doing well." Jim wasn't breaking his salary principles for anyone, and obviously he thought I was too expensive.

My time at Morton was mixed, but we did meet the goals we had been set of selling a player every year. Obviously, though, Allan and I had our football goals which we were determined to achieve, despite regularly selling our greatest players. It was tough, though—Morton fans will remember how we let top players go out on trial during a league run-in when we were in with a great chance of promotion to the top division.

We did have football success, though, and it started straight after I arrived with promotion to the Premier League by winning the old First Division. That came on the last game of the season, one of those where you think you've blown it with a defeat, in this case away to Airdrie. Just when we thought we had thrown away the league title, word came through that our challengers, Dunfermline, had lost away to Montrose.

A couple of relegations followed, but that gave us the opportunity to win another league title. We won the Second Division with a game to spare in what was a pretty competitive league.

All in all, I had a great 10 years at Morton, from 1986 to 1996, that came to an end when we got a new owner. With our previous goal of selling a player every year proving successful, we had made Morton one of the few clubs in Britain that was in the black. Football clubs had for so long been loss-making entities, often the plaything of someone with a spare few bob in the bank. The commercialisation that we see today hadn't fully taken place, so our achievement in keeping the club afloat without the owner, John Wilson, pumping money in was huge. That, of course, also made us interesting to potential buyers, and the club was sold.

The change in ownership made a huge difference to the club, and none of it was positive. Although John Wilson at times had been guilty of sticking his nose in too far to the football side of the club, we always knew he had the best interests of the club at heart. Allan McGraw was great at managing him too 'managing upwards', another fantastic leadership talent. Mr Wilson had criticised Allan following a particular match, and just before the next one he suggested to Allan that he had picked the wrong team. Allan kept his cool and gave the chairman a piece of paper offering him the chance to write down what team he thought that he should pick for the next game. The chairman took the bit of paper, got his pen down and quickly rattled off his team for the game and handed it to Allan. Allan had a look at it and tried not to smile too much. "That's not a bad team, Chairman," he told him. "It's got a great chance of winning the game, but unfortunately football teams consist of eleven starting players, not twelve as you have written down." It was a perfect put down by Allan, and although the chairman might have learnt his lesson from it other members of the board still wanted to interfere.

I was next to be challenged, this time by one of the directors, who decided for himself that my training methods might not be good enough and the players may not have been fit enough, so he invited a well-known local athlete, the great Bill Stoddart, along to assess what we were doing. Bill, a Scottish champion and latterly world record holder in the veteran age group categories, turned up and had a look at the work we were doing on the training ground; 60-metre back-to-back sprints and long diagonals across the pitch were always core exercises for me. After just one session he went back to see the director to let him know that we did not need his help, as we knew what we were doing. Our fitness levels were exceptional.

The new chairman, however, was a completely different kettle of fish. He was determined to try to micromanage every aspect of the club, and, to many on the outside as well as within the club, it looked like this was intended for his own gain. He was a man who nearly broke one of the oldest clubs in Scotland, running it into the ground. I'd had enough of his interference long before he got to that stage, though, and I decided to move on. Scouting for an English Premier League club awaited.

It took a few years to get there, though. I helped out with the scouting back at Aberdeen when Ebbe Skovdahl was the manager. Ebbe was a fantastic man, who the fans loved despite the early league struggles under him. It was great for me to be able to try to give a bit back to the club, writing reports and identifying players. In the ever-changing world that is football, though, that job only lasted so long, so after a brief spell supporting my former protégé Derek McInnes at St Johnstone, I was off to England.

Dave Leadbetter was the head scout at Middlesbrough and he wanted me to join him there. That was my introduction to the English system and a great opportunity to see the future England manager, Gareth Southgate, then in charge of Boro, at first hand. He was another good man who I always thought had enough about him to be successful, and he's done a great job with his national team.

Despite a lot of good work by Southgate, Middlesbrough were relegated and then, as often happens, and would happen again, that starts a chain reaction of changes. Gareth left and my old mate Gordon Strachan came in to replace him. Gordon wanted his own team, so Dave Leadbetter left the club and headed for Swansea City, with their fantastic new Liberty Stadium. They were showing signs of ambition to get to the top flight. Once again Dave asked me to join him, so I moved there to look after scouting in Scotland for Swansea. One of the highlights during my time with Swansea was the quality of some of the managers they had. Brendan Rodgers was there initially, prior to earning his move to Liverpool. I introduced him to a few bits of Scottish football terminology; he was reading one of my reports on a player and came back to me to ask what I meant when I said the player 'slept with the lights on'. He laughed his head off when I explained that it meant he maybe wasn't the bravest player in the world!

Brendan's success with the Swans in the Premier League earned him his big move to Anfield. His replacement was a huge name. The Danish superstar Michael Laudrup came in as manager and had a great first season, culminating with Swansea winning the League Cup and finishing in a solid ninth place in the Premier League. Laudrup, coincidentally, was the nephew of Ebbe Skovdahl, the former Aberdeen manager. That success didn't last, though, and neither did the manager. In fact, none of the subsequent managers lasted very long, with the club ultimately being relegated back to the Championship in 2018. At that point, and after the club had been taken over, the chairman, Huw Jenkins, resigned and the club hired the up-and-coming Graham Potter as the new head coach.

When Potter came in, he wanted a clean slate with all of his own trusted team in place to build back towards the Premier League. That meant the end for the scouting team under (and including) Dave Leadbetter, so another chapter in my football career ended. It was one, though, that I can look back on fondly. Huw Jenkins was an excellent chairman who I really liked. I had initially been working on a non-contract basis, but after a couple of years Mr Jenkins took me into his office and told me that I was a key part of the team and that he wanted me to become a permanent employee. That meant I got to travel to France and Spain on scouting missions, which certainly beat a cold, wet December night at the Falkirk Stadium!

Having said that, I did spend many a cold, wet December, January, February, March, April and May night at the Falkirk Stadium! The manager there, Alex Smith, was a great football man. A close confidant of Fergie's, he had been on hand for him on the odd occasions when the Boss was having his football troubles, including during his first few difficult months with Manchester United. Alex was a wise owl in the football world and a great believer in promoting youth. With my goal being to find inexpensive young talent for Swansea to buy, develop and support the first team and then sell on for a profit, Falkirk was always a great place for me to go. Swansea signed four or five players from Falkirk for very little money, with the biggest success probably being Stephen Kingsley. Signed as a 20-year-old, he moved on to Hull City a few years later for a reputed fee of £3.5 million. The left back with a sweet left foot now also has a couple of Scotland caps to his name.

Jay Fulton, a midfielder, was another who moved to Wales at the age of 19 for very little money and has been a regular in the team over the last few seasons. Of course, though, not every player that a scout identifies is successful and some that you identify don't get picked up by your club. If only they had listened to me about a certain Andy Robertson, now one of the greatest left backs in the world.

Andy was already a superstar by the time my colleague from Swansea, Tim Henderson, who undertook player analysis, moved from Swansea to Championship side Cardiff City, and he wanted me involved again. By this time I hadn't long finished helping out David Hopkin, another ex-Morton youth that I had coached, during his short spell as manager of Bradford City. My time at Cardiff was a bit different, though, as the Covid pandemic had struck and getting to watch games wasn't so easy. I helped out for a few months, keeping an eye mainly on Scottish games, but by this time I was struggling to get around consistently. Old injuries from my playing days were having a lasting impact, and a series of operations on my ankle made it difficult to get around. Hopefully my most recent one will help me to get active again, but my opportunity to visit various football grounds meant that I couldn't really do much scouting after Covid.

I still get to games whenever I can, though, and would never say never to a return to football in some capacity. However, not working in football has allowed me to work on this book, developing the thoughts and stories that I have been putting together with my colleagues over the last few years while out talking to the business world. I've also been having a great time taking my collection of strips and memorabilia to meet the fans. It's been a great opportunity to look back at everything that I have experienced and achieved.

CHAPTER 16
Reflection

THE PROFESSIONAL WORLD OF football does not allow much time for looking back. The old adage 'You're only as good as your last game' pretty much captures it. You were always looking ahead to the next game.

When I moved on from football, delivering workshops and presentations at first required recalling facts and stories from my career—from that we could try to help the attendees learn lessons that they could apply to their own activities.

The process of putting this book together has, however, allowed me to look back and reflect on what is important to me and the impact that my career has had upon me.

I was, and still am, a relatively shy person. Whilst pushy people are generally not liked, I paid the price for being too polite in my early years at Aberdeen.

In football, as in life in general, people have their favourites. Merit alone is not a guarantee for success. I was not a favourite of the management team during my first three or four years. I reckon that I lost out on over 100 first team games, and despite going on to play well over 300 games, that still hurts to this day. Ironically, though, being sent out on loan to the semi-professional Highland League club Peterhead FC was a great experience and stood me in good stead when I did get my chance for first team football upon returning to Aberdeen.

Inwardly, though, during my time at Peterhead, I retained great confidence in my own ability. This was validated during the times that I would train at Pittodrie. I was always one of the first players picked when the senior players were putting sides together for practice matches. These guys wanted to win everything, remember, so they prioritised getting who they thought were the best players. I seemed to fit into that category.

The turning point for me came when Billy McNeill, the former Celtic captain, took over the manager's position. It was much later when I found out that Billy's assistant, John Clark, himself a European Cup Winner, had been following my performances when I was playing in the reserves.

John had told Billy, "John McMaster is a bit of a player." Anyone who is familiar with football in Scotland will know that particular understated expression is the highest accolade you can get! It's a bit like the Yorkshire phrase, 'That'll do,' which really means 'That's fantastic'. High praise indeed!

Apart from the serious injury that I received, my career, went onwards and upwards from that first handshake.

There were other things, though, that assisted in my progression. I made true friends with many great and genuine people. Our kit man/trainer/bus driver/reserve team coach (I could go on!), Teddy Scott, was one of them. My wife, Katy, and I didn't have any family in Aberdeen and at one point we were sleeping on somebody's floor. We then progressed to a bed and breakfast. What would today's superstars make of that? Later, after we moved in to our flat in Summerfield, we needed a three-piece suite, but we didn't have enough credit history to buy it. Teddy Scott stepped in and became our guarantor, which allowed us to get it, and thanks to him, we had something comfortable to sit on! That is true friendship that lasts a lifetime. Just one of the many good deeds by Teddy, and not just for me.

There were no contracts between Teddy and myself. No expectations about getting a return for the risk that he took, just purely and simply a good turn for a friend and colleague who needed some help.

This was prevalent throughout Aberdeen FC at all levels. It had an outcome, though. The one that you can't buy or negotiate. The outcome was one of trust. This trust was there during games. We trusted each other to do our jobs, to help a struggling colleague and to give and take criticism when due.

I have learned that trust is a difficult thing to get. I think that a lot of people believe that it is the hard targets that make things happen. Trust is seen as a soft type of behaviour, but looking back, very few teams succeed at the top purely on technical skills, targets, tactics and so on. They are absolutely necessary but are not enough to get you to the very, very top and keep you there. Outside of football, look at how many top companies, organisations or governments fall apart, not because of their strategy or policies, but because of a complete lack of trust between the individuals at the top of the organisations.

Reflecting has allowed me to appreciate what I have achieved. I am now not just proud of my medals and achievements, but I am proud to talk about them. This is because talking about them allows me to share my personal experiences with others, which will hopefully help them personally. I used to be embarrassed about being called a legend, but not anymore. Not because I want to boast, but rather I can talk factually about what it really takes to get to the top—trust.

Having to present your story gives you a great perspective on what is important, and interestingly this has given me enthusiasm and confidence to learn new things and skills. With help from my colleagues, I have even been able to map my football experience playing, coaching and scouting onto an academic qualifications standard that looks at work-based skills and experience against formal education awards. This has indicated that I am at a level equivalent to MSc, a Master of Science. Maybe we'll just call it a McMaster of Soccer!

So what have I learnt?

Believe in yourself and no apologies for repeating—trust.

CHAPTER 17
The Business Parallels

THROUGHOUT THIS STORY I have spoken about my experiences playing under Sir Alex Ferguson, his influence upon me as a player and as a person and on Aberdeen Football Club in achieving so much success. I have carried these experiences forward with me ever since my playing career finished, and they have been enriched through meeting many business people. Their individual and collective inputs have helped me to appreciate that business can learn from my time as a professional footballer and, particularly, those experiences while I was a player with Aberdeen and during my life after the Dons, be it as a coach, assistant manager or scout.

Much of this book is a football story and my life story, but within that there are the lessons that I learnt that can let you draw some business-related conclusions. Much of this will be useful in any arena, including personal self-development. There is so much theory out there today about the right way to lead and the right way to manage. I don't think that the Boss had any formal training way back then; however, he knew from his younger life on the tough streets of Govan and from his time and experience in the shipyards how to connect with people. Much of what he did can be mapped to some of the theory that people are teaching these days. Even if not, though, you can still read this book and understand what he did and how he was massively successful. Doesn't that beat theory every time?

If I draw a very early conclusion, it was his strength and ability to connect with people that made the difference.

No fancy theories.

No graphs or charts.

Simply the ability to connect with all those that he came into contact with to achieve a common vision.

In my book I have introduced you to some really nice words, and I make no excuses, as today those fancy words reinforce what he did at that time in the history of Aberdeen Football Club.

Clearly, our success came from the team working well in what were some challenging times. The book refers to psychological safety, possibly the most surprising aspect of what we had at Aberdeen given the Boss's public persona. He built an environment that, probably without us realising it at the time, allowed everyone involved in the team to play their part in our success. For example, the Boss let us say what we had to say and we always felt safe and comfortable to express ourselves. There was a time and a place, of course, but he would listen, and he would change if need be. Of course, the final decision was always down to the Boss, but each of us knew that it was safe to put our opinions forward and that we were being listened to.

In business today I believe that leadership is a key part of driving success, and that includes, as I mentioned above, the ability of the leader to allow the free flow of communication at many levels, and in doing that allowing individuals to feel part of the decision-making process. To buy into this aspect is far easier when you feel part of the journey.

Of course, though, having a psychologically safe environment does not necessarily mean a free for all where it becomes in any way abused, abusive or negative. It is a more controlled and managed situation that brings the players in your team together to achieve a common goal with the degree of latitude that allows them to have their say.

That common goal was absolutely vital to us and should be to any organisation, or even to an individual looking for self-improvement. Without a common goal, how can a team or a business begin to appreciate or understand where they are going? How can people buy in to something when they don't know what they will get back for their efforts? In our case we knew that the plan was to win trophies. In the Boss's case it was a simpler directive from the board – don't lose money.

Business today requires a roadmap for success. Without a roadmap there is little chance of success, in my opinion, and I believe that most organisations, while saying they each have a roadmap, have not clearly articulated what that journey looks like to their workforce. When that is the case, the organisation, big or small, won't have a clear, common set of goals that everyone is working towards. The direction can be wayward, confusing and damaging for success.

I mentioned in an earlier chapter about SMART objectives: objectives for the business that are specific in what is to be achieved; measurable in that as we travel on the journey, we can measure our successes and achievement. We need to make people accountable for their part in achieving the roadmap (your journey) and realistic, not over-enthusiastic or unachievable. And finally, to be timebound—achievable within a realistic timeframe.

Having strategic goals in a business is very much part of the SMART process above. For a business to consider a three- or five-year plan, it should be realistic and provide a longer-term view of what can be achieved. Although these can seem a long way off and at a very high level, you need to understand your ultimate goal. This is where you want to get to, and the roadmap will supply the route to it. These strategic objectives are the longer-term plans to grow and develop the business. We didn't try to win a European trophy in our first season under the Boss; he knew that we could get there but also that we needed time to grow and develop. There were many steps on that roadmap that included improving the squad through coaching, building a youth system and making astute transfers, developing the mentality and bringing the whole club together as one.

From the strategic goals you develop the tactical goals, which further drive down the targets into more manageable chunks. From here we are looking at a series of mini wins. Taking it a step further, you have your operational goals, which break down the tactical goals even further and are the beginning of the road to achieving the strategic goal. For us, we had to win our personal battles on the pitch, which allowed us to win matches, which allowed us to win trophies.

All of that might sound a bit drawn out, maybe even complex, but it's not really. When you put it into the SMART context it's very straightforward. For us at Aberdeen Football Club, we may not have had SMART objectives as such—in fact we had never heard of them before but we knew from the Boss that every season our aims were to win more trophies than the previous season—be a one-trophy team, a two-trophy team, then a three-trophy team.

If you looked at a typical season for us as an example, our SMART objectives would have been:

Specific—the aim was to win two trophies.

Measurable—clear when the two trophies were displayed in our trophy cabinet.

Accountable—with the backroom staff, ground staff, playing staff, in fact, everyone within the club being collectively accountable and everyone play their part—remember the janitor helping to put a man on the moon?

Realistic—the objectives were realistic. It may have been less realistic, though, to say that we would win four trophies every season.

Timebound—of course each season was the time in which to reach the targets.

Winning the two trophies was the strategic goal and part

of the longer-term roadmap to win three trophies. Our tactical goals would have included getting results each week to achieve a league position that kept us in contention—we would review and evaluate each month of the season where we were in relation to the plan. Our operational goals were all about winning the match that day, winning our individual battles on the pitch, silencing the crowd at an away game. Week by week, game by game, we planned what we needed to do.

In other words, we had all the daily stuff at the bottom end that were our operational goals. Half way up we had the tactical goals and at the very top the strategic goal.

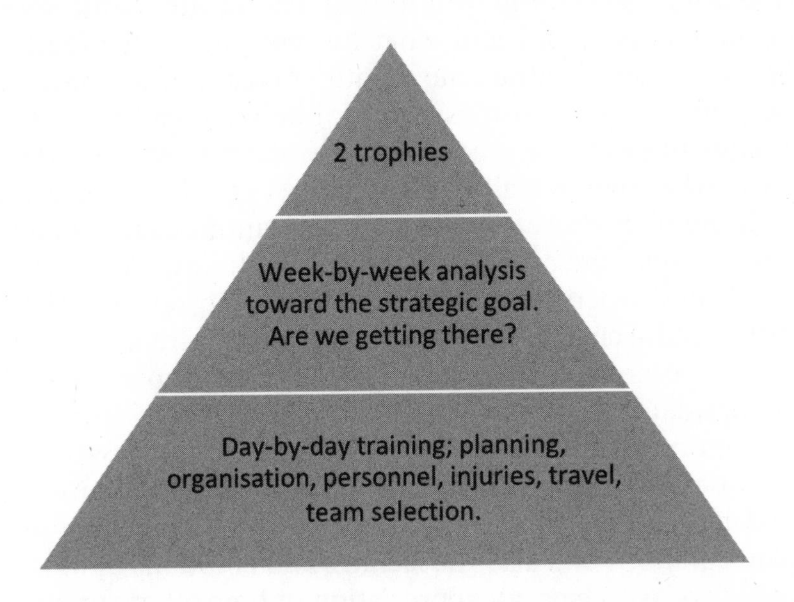

Without a sense of purpose there is little direction for the organisation and, most importantly, no sense of direction for those people that work within it. If it is a case of simply accepting 'second best' or 'things as they are', then motivation and drive may wane, with people becoming disenfranchised and disillusioned with the business. People will turn up for work and do their job, put in their eight hours each day. But with nothing to strive towards, how can the business progress? Key people who do have the drive to succeed will get frustrated and leave, weakening the organisation and strengthening your competitor's advantage.

Another of Fergie's major strengths was his fantastic ability to connect with people, part of what we now know as emotional intelligence. This connection between people, from everything that I've seen, is vital to success. The Boss had the skillset to be able to interact with all those that he came into contact with at every level. From Bella the tea lady, whom the Boss would chat with daily, to Mr Donald the chairman, he would take time for everyone to make them know that they mattered. In doing this he formed a connection with all of those around him, helping him to understand them and them to understand him and what he required. It helped the Boss to understand the subtle behavioural changes, which in today's business world, I believe is a key part of leadership.

I think that we all can perhaps sense the changes in behaviour of those around us in our immediate families, for example, and especially so with our children; when they are happy, when they are sad. So, if we can relate to those behavioural changes in our families and children, then why are we sometimes not similarly tuned in to those we work alongside?

Emotional intelligence is the nice modern business phrase that describes how we understand our own emotions as a person, how aware we are of our own individual feelings and emotions and also the feelings and emotions of others. It allows us to have an appreciation of how others perceive us as individuals and, by being aware of it, allows us to appreciate the feelings and character of others. It's about how we impact on others and make others feel and, more importantly, about our relationship management with those we come into contact with.

One of my colleagues has told me his story about when he was going through his training to become a Royal Air Force Officer. He hasn't forgotten much of that training, or the impact it had on him as a person. He was seated in the middle of a circle made up his colleagues, who each in turn had to consider what his good qualities were and also what his not-so-great qualities were. They then had to tell him about both. It was called a Critical Analysis Group (CAG), and, although this was appropriate for the Air Force, it won't necessarily be the correct approach for you. However, it does show that sometimes it is good to ask the people around you, "How am I doing as your boss?" This will give you some vital feedback, but be prepared to receive the good and not-so-good examples of how you are working. It can be a great way to understand yourself, allowing you to improve by working on your own emotional intelligence.

This approach can be strengthened with another technique that involved two-way dialogue around performance that could work at all levels. Sets of two people from within a work group would be paired together and each would ask the following questions to the other:

1. How do I help you?

2. How do I hinder you?

3. How can we work better together?

After the first person has asked the questions and received the feedback, the positions are swapped and the process repeated with the second person asking the same questions.

The discussions that this process generates helps each individual to appreciate their understanding of themselves and of others as well, and ultimately, it builds a higher level of emotional intelligence. It led to major behavioural change and, notably, the honest feedback greatly improved the level of trust between the staff.

A lot of scientific research has gone into emotional intelligence, and the work of Dan Goleman is very good. It's impossible to summarise the complete findings in one or two sentences, but clearly those supervisors, managers and leaders who are able to show emotional intelligence are more likely to succeed. This was particularly evident at Aberdeen Football Club under the Boss, as it was at every club where he worked.

The Boss knew everyone; he understood them and he could relate to them. Did he get it right all the time? Of course not; who ever does in life? However, my experience of working with him, combined with what we know now, has shown the depth of emotional intelligence that he possessed.

There are several other facets to emotional intelligence that I could begin to suggest were evident, such as his drive, his motivation and his empathy, but I truly believe that his self-awareness and his ability to listen to others were the catalysts for our successes. He had the ability to inspire and transform others through his people skills. Again, this is what he did and we know the results he got. The theory just supports his actions.

So, throughout the book I have tried to express not only his influence on me as a player but also his influence upon the club, the environment and the entire city.

Business today can be a real challenge, whether at the start-up phase or at in established operation. We work in a multi-cultural environment and in a more competitive, pressurised environment, and I strongly believe that businesses need to consider their leadership skills as the foundation for operational success. It's really not rocket science in my opinion and just perhaps needs a change in the mindset of many to give greater value to the people that work for you or with you.

What we saw at Aberdeen, and I'm sure it's common throughout business and life in general, is that things settle into a pattern of acceptance. With that, over time we each individually create our assumptions of how things are, and that can influence our way of thinking. Not all of this will be bad; to move forward we need to challenge ourselves to find other ways in which to operate.

If the Boss had simply accepted that we were doing OK when he took over at Aberdeen Football Club, I wouldn't be able to tell my story. If the players, as they possibly did prior to his arrival, accepted that to be second best was the norm, then again, I wouldn't be able to tell my story.

Change is uncomfortable sometimes but can be palatable if undertaken with both a proactive and a challenging mindset. It will happen best if you take the people along with you, showing them where you are going and what the rewards are. Not everyone is the same, so getting that 'buy in' will require an understanding of these differences and managing them.

So how do I summarise this?

For me the key is to have a clear common goal or objective. To communicate that common goal to all and allow the individuals to each use their skills and knowledge to great effect. On the journey, sprinkle all the aforementioned with a bit of emotional intelligence. Think about the easy things that Fergie did and the massive impact they had; the chats with all the staff, incorporating everyone into the goals and the successes. Make sure that everyone understands that they have been a huge part of the successes through little rewards (like being part of the team photograph). This is where the trust is built, when you know that everyone is committed to the vision and will give their all to achieve it.

There is talk of being 'intelligently disruptive', and I too think that in this book, my personal story has encountered a great leader who was intelligently disruptive, but he was possibly unaware that he was being so. Your goals have to be achievable but need to stretch you at the same time, otherwise you will stagnate. That will involve change somewhere along the line, so look for what you can disrupt. That's where the big gains can come.

Much of it is very simple and straightforward. Most of it will make up a long and complicated business course that explains what is required. For me, though, I look at two things; I look at what the greatest leader most of us know actually did and I look at the medals in my collection and what he achieved everywhere that he went. The proof, as they say, is in the pudding.

Over the last few years I've been taking this message

out to businesses, and many of them have received it very well and implemented a lot of what I've talked about in this book. Major oil companies had me talking to their crews on oil rigs, building their teams before they set off to drill in the oil fields around the country. I've presented to a European-wide body representing some top accountancy firms, and my message has also been delivered to students studying for their Master of Business degrees, and with not too many challenging what I have been saying. I hope that it serves you well if you go on to use it in your business or personal life.

EPILOGUE
Dewy Eyed Romanticism

SO, THE BOSS WAS incredibly successful as manager of Aberdeen Football Club. One of the things that I love to tell people when I'm doing my leadership coaching is that sometimes you don't need to look at the theory, the academic stuff. I'm not great with that myself, which is why I surround myself with people who do know what it is all about. What I say to people is, "Look at the medals, look at what we won, what he won." Look at the sustainability of it—he wasn't lucky, or at least he wasn't just lucky.

We hadn't won a league title in decades before Fergie arrived; we won three in eight years with him. Domestic cups came along virtually every year during that period too, and of course European success following, leading to us being labelled arguably the greatest club team in the world.

But maybe Aberdeen were just becoming the great club they always should have been? So what happened in the years after Sir Alex left the club in 1986?

Aberdeen had an excellent cup double in the 1989/90 season under the guidance of the great Alex Smith. They won the League Cup twice after that, but there hasn't been another league title since Fergie left the club. Meanwhile, of course, we've seen his record at Manchester United and what's happened since he left them. Man United, Aberdeen, Black Eyed Peas and Prince Andrew all have this one thing in common—they've all been hopeless since Fergie left!

It's also worth looking at how his influence rubbed off on his players. This is what happened to the rest of the Gothenburg Greats:

Jim Leighton
The only Aberdeen player signed directly by Fergie when he joined Manchester United in 1988. He won an FA Cup winners' medal in 1990, although his United career didn't end well following a high-profile fall out with the Boss. On his return to Scotland, he got back into the Scottish national team and racked up 91 appearances for his country, playing until he was in his 40s.

Doug Rougvie
Big Doug earned a glamour move to Chelsea in 1984 before winning lower league promotions with Brighton and Montrose, where he also started his management career. He got a cap for Scotland, something that I didn't, and Stuart Kennedy never lets me forget!

Stuart Kennedy
Should be me here, but that's all been covered. Stuart deserved to be playing on that fantastic night but for his career-ending injury. Stuart only got capped eight times for Scotland, which was a travesty, but with Rangers' Sandy Jardine and Celtic's Danny McGrain as competition, it was never going to be easy. Since retiring, Stuart hasn't been involved in the game and has been running his own successful businesses.

Willie Miller
One of Scotland's greatest ever footballers, he played over 60 times for his country in an era when we were incredibly well off for great central defenders. Willie went on to manage Aberdeen before being appointed to the board of directors, later becoming Director of Football. He is now one of the most prominent football analysts in the country.

Alex McLeish
Alongside Willie for club and country, Big Eck formed a formidable partnership. He has enjoyed a successful management career north and south of the border, including five trophies with Rangers in just three seasons

and a winning rare piece of silverware for Birmingham City when they lifted the League Cup in the 2010/11 season. Two successful spells as Scotland manager followed that included a victory in Paris against France and winning the Nations League section, setting Scotland up for their first appearance at a major tournament for years.

Neale Cooper
The much loved and sadly missed Tattie, as we knew him. Managed several clubs in Scotland and England, winning a league title and promotion with Ross County and achieving legendary status for a second time, this time with Hartlepool United.

Neil Simpson
Big Simmie moved to Newcastle in 1990 and then Motherwell before finishing his playing career at Cove Rangers. He has been head of Aberdeen's youth development since 2011, bringing through the next crop of youngsters.

Gordon Strachan
Gordon was already at Manchester United when the Boss arrived at Old Trafford and had added an FA Cup winner's medal to his collection. He decided to step down a division to join Leeds United in 1989 and helped them win the Second Division title and promotion. Within two years he had captained them as they won the First Division, the top flight of English football. He then went into management and had great success, at first relative to the size of the clubs he managed, such as Coventry and Southampton, and latterly by winning several trophies as manager of Celtic. Another ex-colleague of mine who would manage Scotland.

Peter Weir
Another great player who was somehow only capped six times by Scotland. Moved to Leicester City when he left Aberdeen, followed by a spell as coach at Celtic, but has been back at the club since working with the youth development set-up.

Mark McGhee
Dingus went on to win many more trophies with Celtic and had a successful playing spell with Newcastle before going into management. As a manager, Mark has had more clubs than Tiger Woods, winning promotion with three different clubs in England.

Eric Black
Blackie moved to France to play with Metz after leaving Aberdeen, where he won the Summer Cup and the French Cup. Sadly, he was forced to retire criminally early due to injury. He had good spells in management with Motherwell and Coventry City, plus a host of jobs as assistant manager in the top two divisions in England.

John Hewitt
The super-sub who scored the winning goal in Gothenburg has largely been out of the game since retiring, apart from a brief spell as manager of Dundalk and assistant manager at Cove Rangers.

I'm sure a look at his Manchester United players would show a similar progression into management, with plenty achieving success. Although I do wonder if anyone has fully picked up exactly what Sir Alex had? I'll leave that one open for debate.

Acknowledgements

THERE ARE A LOT of people from a lot of different parts of my life that I need to thank, from my home life and growing up, school, football and life after football, including the writing of this book.

I have to start with my parents, Susan and John—Sissy and Miffy, as they were known—for giving me a great start in life. Through the difficult times and beyond, following the loss of my father, my sisters and brother were with me all the way: Ina, Bridgett, Mary, Theresa, Jean, Susan and Andrew. Sadly, only Theresa and Susan are still around, but none have been forgotten—they would have been so proud to read this, and we miss them all. I also had a very important uncle, Andrew McKillop, who was a huge support after the loss of my dad at such a young age.

Growing up led to me having my own family, and their support has never wavered. My wife, Katy, has been by my side for 50 years and has been fantastic for me, plus she's given me 3 great sons in John, Steven and Scott, whom we love dearly. And we also have our grandson, Liam, who is gold dust for us—and not a bad footballer either!

I need to mention a few other people too who've helped me to get where I ended up. My teacher, Dave Allan, who looked after the school team and instilled great confidence in me by making me captain. It felt great at that age to have my ability recognised. After school, Alex McKenzie and Campbell O'May, who ran the Port Rovers under 16s and 18s, continued my development, along with the under 21s manager, Tommy Mooney. There was also my Boys' Brigade captain, John McKenzie, who helped with life lessons as well as giving me another opportunity to play the game that I loved.

Of course, who knows where I would have ended up had it not been for John McNab scouting me on the Port Glasgow playing fields at Parklea, but thankfully he saw me and got me my move to Aberdeen. I need to mention chief scout Bobby Calder too, of course, who took John's advice and looked at me.

From there, all of the managers that I played for had

a big hand in my development and in my life, even when there were the inevitable disappointments. Playing for Jimmy Bonthrone, Ally MacLeod, Billy McNeill with John Clark and, of course, the Boss, Alex Ferguson, along with the brilliant Archie Knox, was a huge honour—what a list! And I thank each of them for every opportunity I was given. Amongst that, of course, are my great memories of a season on loan at Peterhead in the Highland League.

I would like to mention Ally Begg for the help and support he gave to us when he was working with Saltire in Qatar.

Of course I will never forget the great Teddy Scott, who treated me like a son and was always there for my family and me. What a great guy he was. He was the heart and soul of that great family club, which was excellently led by the chairman, Mr Donald, along with Chris Anderson and Ian Donald.

There are a huge bunch of people who have helped me with this book. Sean Wallace from the *Aberdeen Press and Journal/Evening News*, who provided advice and guidance at the start of the process. Big shout out also to Neil Drysdale, who came up with the book title! I also got great advice from Callum McFadden for pointers around social media and also the introduction to our publishers, Mathew Mann and Barrie Pierpoint at Morgan Lawrence. Thanks to Lee Clark for the cover, to Lois Hide and Catherine Dunn for editing and proofreading, and Harry Worgan for the marketing. Thanks also to Paul Kelly who shared his own book writing experiences.

This book would have been much more difficult to get published without the support of our sponsors, so a huge thank you to them: David McRae from Just Employment Law, Bob Bain, Jock Gardiner and Chris Gavin from the Aberdeen FC Heritage Trust, Duncan Moir of McLeod+Aitken, and my good friend Raymond Gray of Pier Solutions.

And finally, to the brilliant Spain-based sports journalist Graham Hunter for writing the foreword to the book. I couldn't have asked for anything better from a very special friend.

I will no doubt remember dozens of other great people who have helped me as soon as this book goes to the publisher, so a thank you to all. Special mention, of course, to all the Dons fans for their support over the years. I'll see you all about!

Thank You To Our Sponsors

This book is only possible because of the generous support from our sponsors.

Aberdeen Football Club Heritage Trust

ABERDEEN FOOTBALL CLUB HERITAGE TRUST is delighted to play a small part in bringing John's story to print.

Riding high in Aberdeen's all-time appearances chart, McMaster was a key player in the 1980s successes but spanned much of the 1970s too. He currently sits 24th by that measure and with 33 goals is also a top 100 scorer. His development into an influential player, boosted by a spell playing in the Highland League, came mainly under Ally MacLeod and Billy McNeill, and gradually he converted from a winger to an influential left -sided midfielder thanks to McNeill.

Supporters recognised that John was an integral part of the successful Ferguson team, overlooked by Scotland but adding impressive creativity domestically. His defence-splitting passes brought goals for his fellow Dons and joy to the terraces. When he won the ball, the crowd knew that something worthwhile could happen, from one of those passes to a long-range goal, even when he had slotted in at left back.

Less noted by some, John was a real club man, and when he was prevented from playing because of lengthy spells of injury, he helped with the reserve team, both at matches and training, as well as coaching the under 13s.

His value to the Dons and to football was underlined when a galaxy of British stars turned out for his testimonial match, as did a crowd of 16,500 admiring fans.

When it comes to looking at the heritage of Aberdeen Football Club, John McMaster stands shoulder to shoulder with the club's greatest players, leaving cherished memories of great achievements and a great player.

McLeod+Aitken

THREE DAYS AFTER MY 18th birthday I took the first ever plane journey of my life and flew to Gothenburg in Sweden. The date was 11 May 1983, and it turned out to be the most famous night in the history of Aberdeen Football Club, with a 2-1 victory in the European Cup Winners' Cup against the mighty Real Madrid.

One of the many stars that night for the Dons was John McMaster, playing at left back. Here we are, 40 years later and finally getting the chance to read the memoirs of this gifted footballer and all-round nice guy. I am fortunate as a life-long Dons fan to be able to call John my friend. We have shared many great occasions and he has always been so engaging, telling great stories of the glory days, with his numerous medals close to hand to proudly show round.

McLeod+Aitken, since their formation in 1954, have always supported Aberdeen Football Club. Many of the directors and staff are season ticket holders and shareholders, and McLeod+Aitken regularly sponsor home matches at Pittodrie.

As quantity surveyors and project managers McLeod+Aitken have carried out many projects for Aberdeen Football Club, including the Richard Donald Stand and the Cormack Park Training Complex.

McLeod+Aitken, and myself personally, wish John the very best of luck with his autobiography.

Duncan Moir
Managing Director
www.mcleod-aitken.com

McLeod+Aitken

Just Employment Law

"Aberdeen have what money can't buy; a soul, a team spirit built in a family tradition."

THE AFOREMENTIONED QUOTE FROM the legendary Real Madrid coach Alfredo Di Stéfano, spoken in the aftermath of his team having been defeated by Aberdeen Football Club in the European Cup Winners' Cup Final on 11 May 1983, is an enduring and lingering reminder of what was achieved by a team of Scottish players with raw talent that night in rainy Gothenburg. However, this does not come close to completing the picture.

The Gothenburg Greats of 1983 have left an enduring legacy that transcends, and shall continue to transcend, generations in the northeast of Scotland and beyond. They put Aberdeen firmly on the sporting map and have inspired millions to achieve the seemingly unachievable.

I have been privileged to have met most of the Gothenburg Greats over the years. They say never meet your heroes. I have met mine and regret not a single meeting.

I first met John McMaster many years ago and can state without contradiction that he embodies the full spirit of Gothenburg. He leads by example in his personal and professional life after football, just as he did during his playing days. The leadership traits inherited by so many players who were lucky enough to have worked under Sir Alex Ferguson are strikingly evident in John, who shares these traits with business leaders in his life after football. He does indeed have what money can't buy—a soul and a team spirit with its origins firmly entrenched in a family tradition—and a wand of a left foot!

At Just Employment Law, we are all delighted and proud to partner with John with our sponsorship of his excellent book. A fitting legacy for a true Gothenburg Great. Stand free, John.

David M. McRae
Managing Director
Just Employment Law

Pier Solutions

IT IS A HUGE HONOUR to have the opportunity to sponsor John McMaster's autobiography. Our chairman, Raymond, worked in hospitality extensively during the Gothenburg years and that is when he met John, a talented midfielder playing in a very talented team, who achieved incredible success under the leadership of Sir Alex Ferguson.

I'm a big Manchester United fan, and there has always been a connection between United and Aberdeen because of Sir Alex. I'm a long-time admirer of how Ferguson managed to consistently achieve such great success at his various clubs. This book is slightly different to a typical autobiography because as well as chronicling John's remarkable career, he also describes the leadership techniques that made Sir Alex, and the clubs that he managed, such a dominant force in both Scotland and England.

Here at Pier Solutions we combine innovation with efficient delivery, and we have built a global reputation for excellence. We take the time to understand exact project needs and build a solution that helps you excel.

Our team have a proven track record in delivering customised, container and modular projects. Our in-house design and production team is committed to excellence and building trusted partnerships with our clients.

Our experienced team has an enviable track record of delivering innovative engineered modular and containerised equipment for offshore, onshore and energy transition related solutions.

We are delighted to be supporting this book and wish John every success.

James Walbrin
CEO

Statistics And Honours

	Appearances	Goals
Aberdeen 1972—1987	315	33
Peterhead (Loan) 1972—1973	20	14
Greenock Morton 1987—1988	29	2
Total	**364**	**49**

Honours

Scottish Premier League	Winners	1980, 1984, 1985
Scottish Cup	Winners	1982, 1983, 1984, 1986
Scottish Cup	Runners Up	1978
Scottish League Cup	Winners	1986
Scottish League Cup	Runners Up	1979, 1980
European Cup Winners' Cup	Winners	1983
European Super Cup	Winners	1983
Aberdeen Hall of Fame	Inductee	2017

Meet The Writers

John has collaborated with Robin McAuslan, David Christie and Neil Martin to write this book.

Robin McAuslan

A LEFT-FOOTED, GINGER-HAIRED product of Inverclyde, whose footballing journey started as a left-sided forward before moving into midfield and then left back. And that is where the comparisons with John McMaster and me end. My lack of footballing ability meant that I never progressed beyond the Saturday and Sunday morning local pub leagues, and I managed to make the number 14 jersey my own long before squad numbers existed.

So, sadly, I had to get a proper job. Twenty years of management in a multinational corporation followed before I took some of the skills that I had learned and applied them to my own businesses, which included retail, tourism and business consultancy. Co-author Neil Martin, who I was by then working with, had met John by this time and asked him for some help to open up the Aberdeen area for us to work in. I was well aware of John, having watched my team, Morton, regularly beat that great Aberdeen team, but I also remembered watching that game in Gothenburg in 1983 in the student union when I should have been studying for my final exams.

John's stories, that began just being funny football stories, soon started ringing some bells for us. We were, at that time, running leadership training at various Scottish universities for MBA students. Part of the week's programme involved looking outside business to see what could be learned, including from sport, and here was John suddenly presenting this insight into the methods of one of the greatest leaders that we all know. The rest, as they say, is His Story.

David Christie

THERE IS THE STRONGEST of links between leadership and success in both sport and business, which is rarely addressed.

Co-author David Christie FCMI has had a full, varied career; he's held a commission in the Royal Air Force and run businesses in the private sector as well as working in the public sector supporting entrepreneurs. He maintains that when people connect, be it in business or in sport, performance excellence is achievable.

He met John and fellow co-authors some years ago, and so began the journey to tell to John's life story from Gibshill to Gothenburg, bringing to life those powerful skills that connect people for business performance excellence, as made clear with Aberdeen Football Club under the leadership of the Boss.

The stories that David tells within the book are pragmatic and taken from actual life experiences, highlighting both the good and not-so-good aspects of running a business, recognising that leadership skills, or indeed lack of leadership skills, will without exception impact performance and business excellence. David continues to work throughout the world, sharing his knowledge and experience within many organisations.

Neil Martin

LIKE MOST BOYS OF my generation, I dreamt of being a professional footballer, and like most boys of my generation, dreaming was as far as it got.

My interest in and love of football did, however, lead me to be involved with the administration and in a leading role in a semi-professional football club. This lasted for over three decades.

This was not my main career path. In parallel with my football commitments, I spent those three decades working for a USA multinational in the semiconductor industry, mostly in high-volume, high-tech manufacturing, a corporate environment leading to a senior leadership role. This involved literally hundreds of colleagues across various skillsets, PhD to vocational.

There was, however, a break in the above when I worked in R&D, this time for a competitor. I was brought on board due to my manufacturing experience. The team was small. The core consisted of highly qualified, highly recognised experts in their individual technical fields. All had numerous patents to their name and regularly presented at conferences, etc. My colleagues truly were a collection of world class talented individuals.

Unfortunately, in spite of this world class talent, we failed to meet our goal of turning R&D into a profitable manufacturing business. Why? Well, simply put, and with the benefit of hindsight, we put no value on teamwork. The classic failure of putting talented individuals together with little effort on cohesion and softer skills and expecting outstanding results.

Returning to the main period in my career. At one point

the organisation came under severe attack from a number of sources. Intra-company competition, global competition and even political pressures all contrived to threaten the existence of the organisation. Fortunately we had been putting great emphasis on individual development, teamwork, etc. and, most importantly, how we treated each other as individuals. We survived these onslaughts and indeed more than survived. In a global survey of manufacturing, the organisation was ranked in the top 5%—from survival mode to world class.

This leads me back to my endeavours in semi-professional football. It was through this that I got to know John McMaster. Firstly, our contact was football based, but as circumstances would have it, this led to a journey that has taken us from John presenting to academics as a key presenter in workshops and motivational speaking to the publication of this book.

John's story of overcoming personal challenges to become a key member of the Aberdeen team, led by Sir Alex Ferguson, that beat Real Madrid in the European Cup Winners' Cup final in 1983 is fascinating in itself and a great example of individual resilience and talent.

John's story, however, provides an insight into what in our opinion really gave Aberdeen the edge. It was the highly organised, highly demanding environment developed by Sir Alex. John's story in this book will provide what probably distinguished Aberdeen from its competitors and may well surprise many people. The people in that club, from top to bottom, genuinely cared for each other.

John and my fellow co-authors echo the sentiment that if you truly want to be world class in anything, you really do need to care for each other; that is the secret. If you don't believe that, then listen to the words of one of the greatest footballers ever:

"Aberdeen have what money can't buy; a soul, a team spirit built in a family tradition."
Alfredo Di Stéfano.